FLESH
BONE
WOOD

CHRISTVS·SACERDOS

BUT WIFI ΤΕ PRECIOUS BLOOD ⊕ CHRIST

WHO VERILY WAS FOREORDINED BEFORE ΤΕ FOUNDION

ΤΕ WORLD · YE KNOW FIAT YE WERE NOT REDEEMED WIFI ⊕RRLIPTIBIE THINGS

I · N · R · I

CHRIST OUR PASSOVER
IS SACRIFICED FOR US

LET

Geoffrey Rowell, the Bishop of Basingstoke, is the author of numerous academic and devotional works. Formerly the Chaplain of Keble College, Oxford, he now lives near Alton in Hampshire.

Julien Chilcott-Monk is a writer and musician living in Winchester, Hampshire.

FLESH
BONE
WOOD

Entering into the
mysteries of the Cross

Geoffrey Rowell and
Julien Chilcott-Monk

CANTERBURY
PRESS
Norwich

Copyright © Geoffrey Rowell and Julien Chilcott-Monk 2001

First published in 2001 by
The Canterbury Press Norwich
(a publishing imprint of Hymns Ancient & Modern Limited
a registered charity)
St Mary's Works, St Mary's Plain
Norwich, Norfolk, NR3 3BH

British Library Cataloguing in Publication Data

A catalogue record of this book is available
from the British Library

ISBN 1-85311-380-8

Scriptural quotations are from the Catholic Edition copyright
1965 and 1966 of the Revised Standard Version of the Bible
copyright 1946, 1952 and 1957 by the Division of Christian
Education of the National Council of Churches in the USA.
Used by permission. All Rights Reserved.

Illustrations gratefully received from the private collection of
Julian W. S. Litten: *Keynotes of the Catholic Faith* (Selected
from the Diary and Letters of John A. Le Couteur), Alexander
Moring Ltd, (date unknown), pp. 73, 247; *The People's
Rosary Book*, The Society of SS Peter and Paul, London,
The Anglican Missal, The Society of SS Peter and Paul,
London, 1939, pp. ii, 3, 122.

Typeset by Rowland Phototypesetting Ltd,
Bury St Edmunds, Suffolk
Printed in Great Britain by
Bookmarque, Croydon, Surrey

Contents

Introduction

In John Keble's library, preserved at Keble College, Oxford, there is a small book by the seventeenth-century spiritual writer, Jean-Joseph Surin (1600–65). It was presented to Keble by Edward Pusey as a token of thanks for Keble's ministry as pastor and confessor in one of the darkest moments of Pusey's life. Pusey had found in Surin a Passion-centred spirituality that spoke to his condition. He wrote that Surin 'knew in its inmost depths, what is self-abnegation, and what "the abundance of the consolations" of Christ'. Surin's *Foundations of the Spiritual Life* were 'the direct fruit of the Cross'.[1] This strong thread in Surin's spirituality that spoke to Pusey some two centuries later was a Passion mysticism which drew Surin to focus on the sufferings of Christ as the key to penitence. Thus Surin could write:

> Let us contemplate the mirror of all the penitent saints: Jesus Christ in the Praetorium of Pilate and upon the cross. In the Praetorium he appears as an object of abomination before the whole people, in the ludicrous regalia of a mock king . . . . For since an incarnate God was willing to appear in that state in which Pilate showed him to the people, what point would it have if not to say to men, through his example, what St Ignatius says in his *Constitutions*,

that 'out of gratitude and love for him, we should desire to be reckoned fools and glory in wearing his livery'.[2]

This kind of imaginative contemplation has deep roots in the history of Christian devotion. Surin is an outstanding example, but Ignatius Loyola, whom he quotes, is another, whose contemporary influence has been powerful, but whose earlier influence on patterns of meditation and visualization of the Passion in Herbert, Donne and Crashaw is also notable.[3] As early as the turn of the fifth century John Cassian brought the monastic traditions of the Christian East to the West and in his *Conferences* distilled some of the major themes of the spiritual wisdom he had learnt from the fathers of the desert. In that context, as Owen Chadwick has written, the Bible was studied devotionally rather than critically, searching for 'what it meant obviously for the characters in the Bible; then what it meant for the soul that reads; and finally what it meant for the Church of all time . . . . It was intended more to touch the heart than to inform the head.'[4]

In the first of his *Conferences* Cassian writes that 'the activity of the heart is compared, not inappropriately, to that of a mill which is activated by the circular motion of water'.

The mill cannot cease operations at all so long as it is driven round by the pressure of the water, and it, then, becomes quite feasible for the person in charge to decide whether he prefers wheat or barley or darnel to be ground. And one thing is clear. Only that will be ground which is fed in by the one who is in charge.

To overcome 'the lairs of the wild beasts within us and the hiding places of the venomous serpents' we need every hour and every moment to 'work over the earth of our heart with the plough of Scripture, that is, with the memory of the Lord's cross'.[5]

In the fourteenth century the fire of love that is to be kindled in our hearts is seen as flowing through the Passion of Christ.

The divine fatherly wisdom flows continually through the Passion of our Lord into panting, thirsting hearts which are burned up by the divine fire of love. The first so dries and burns them that they are seized with an excessive thirst, and in this thirst they run with a flaming desire to the streams and to the wounds of our Lord from which all grace flows. To these they hold their mouths and drink.[6]

Lady Julian, Thomas Traherne and Isaac Watts – the last through his communion hymn, 'When I survey the wondrous Cross' – remind us of how universal this imaginative contemplation of the Lord's Passion has been.

Meditation can be described as 'a craft of thinking'.[7] It has always involved picturing as a way of entering into the story of salvation, and ikons, frescoes, stained glass and the very architecture of churches have been called upon to assist in this process. The tradition of beginning an act of meditation or worship with the sign of the cross is very ancient, and the painted cross, whether on the walls of churches, or in the cross-carpet pages of books like the Lindisfarne Gospels (*c.* 698), acted as a visual marker to lead into prayer.[8]

This Lent book therefore stands in a long Christian tradition in providing passages of Scripture, together with imaginative reflections from the Beloved Disciple or others involved in the Lord's Passion, to be doors through which we may enter into the saving mystery of the cross. The short passages of comment challenge us to both further meditation and deeper response. The book ends with Easter, for it is in the light of Easter that the cross is seen as the place where God both plumbed the depth of human evil and also 'reigned and triumphed from the tree'. As two recent writers put it, the Lord 'handed Himself over without limit or reserve – unto death. He entered into the totality or extremity of passion – the situation in which there is no limit to what may be done to one, to what one may receive or suffer.'[9] And for that reason:

> Jesus is still and always Jesus crucified. There is no going back on the crucifixion. Jesus does not want it undone; God does not want it undone, because it is in looking at Jesus crucified that we see him in focus, brought to a still point. And as we get Jesus in focus so we see through him to the heart of God.[10]

And the heart of God is a love that will never let us down and will never let us go.

+ Geoffrey Rowell
September 2000

[1] Cf. John Saward's comparison of Surin and Pusey in *Perfect Fools: Folly for Christ's Sake in Catholic and Orthodox Spirituality*, Oxford University Press, Oxford, 1980, pp. 203ff.

[2] J-J. Surin, Letter to Père Huby, quoted in ibid., p. 141.

[3] J. A. W. Bennett, *Poetry of the Passion: Studies in Twelve Centuries of English Verse*, Clarendon Press, Oxford, 1982, pp. 145 and ff.

[4] Owen Chadwick, Introduction to John Cassian, Conferences (Classics of Western Spirituality), Paulist Press, New York, 1985, p. 22.

[5] Cassian, *Conferences*, I.18, 22, pp. 52, 58.

[6] *The Book of the Poor in Spirit*, quoted in Kenneth Leech, *True prayer: an introduction to Christian Spirituality*, Sheldon Press, London, 1980, p. 38.

[7] Mary Carruthers, *The Craft of Thought: Meditation, rhetoric and the making of images, 400–1200*, Cambridge University Press, Cambridge, 1998, p. 4.

[8] Ibid., p. 168.

[9] W. H. Vanstone, *The Stature of Waiting*, Darton, Longman & Todd, London, 1982, p. 87.

[10] Geoffrey Preston, *Hallowing the Time: Meditations on the Cycle of the Christian Liturgy*, Darton, Longman & Todd, London, 1980, p. 108.

Preface and
how to use this book

It is our hope that this book will encourage a profound
contemplation of the Passion of our Lord during the
season of Lent; but it is not a conventional Lent book
of readings and prayer. For that, the reader must look
elsewhere. The book found its origin in Good Friday
addresses by Bishop Geoffrey Rowell, which had the
title we have given to the book, 'Flesh, Bone, Wood'.
In those addresses, in which the varying viewpoints of
the participants and onlookers in the Passion were
punctuated by three hammer blows on the pulpit, the
congregation was invited to identify with those very
different reactions. This initial starting point has been
expanded to provide a journey into the Passion
throughout Lent. The comments on each meditation
have been drawn from sermons and addresses by
Bishop Geoffrey.

'Flesh, Bone, Wood' is, therefore, a series of spiritual
exercises on the Passion. As such it is related to both
the imaginative, meditative tradition of Ignatian spirituality and the much older tradition of memory and
meditation explored in the Introduction by Bishop
Geoffrey. Daily, the reader is invited to stand beside –
or, indeed, in the shoes of – the Beloved Disciple and
others as the crucifixion slowly takes place. This exer-
cise is followed by a passage from one or more of the

Gospels, which, occasionally, appears to be a 'flash-back' prompted by a thought expressed in the soliloquy. From these passages unfold the narratives of the Passion. And to all this will be brought the reader's own understanding in the knowledge and light of the Resurrection. In consequence, a picture of the Passion emerges from three different perspectives – as it were from three different camera angles. For as long as time allows, the mind ought to be given free rein to enter completely into the drama and pain of the Passion, which is at one with the pain and suffering of a fallen world. And yet, at the heart of the Passion is the mystery of our salvation and healing.

Comment, and a point or question for application, self-examination or consideration, are then provided: the first to elucidate or to open a door to other lines of enquiry; the second not only to stand alone as genuinely arising from what has gone before but also to serve as a mnemonic with which the reader can associate the various strands of the day's contemplation. Three psalms thread their way through Lent, verse by verse (130, 22, 93).

It is entirely a matter for the reader, but it is suggested that the daily session begin in prayer – for example, the Gloria Patri and the Paternoster – and end in prayer – for example, an Ave Maria and the Collect of the day. However, something less formal and less rigid may be preferred. To assist in the work of contemplation it is helpful to have set before one a cross or crucifix or an ikon or painting of the Passion.

Julien Chilcott-Monk

ASH
WEDNESDAY
TO SATURDAY

Ash Wednesday

The Beloved Disciple (on arrival at Golgotha):

I am watching the final stages of a nightmare. The past hours have made it clear that this hideous drama has now taken on a momentum of its own as though beyond any human control; yes, beyond the control of any of the players: of Annas, Caiaphas, Herod, Pilate, or even Caesar himself. The Master's equanimity seems to be a painful resignation, almost contentment, even in his agony. I do not understand. I feel anger, frustration and sorrow; but these emotions mingle and fight for supremacy. Before Pilate, he was clearly of equal intellect, if not indeed in command of the situation, though he ought to have been cowed. Is this the courage obtained through the selfless acceptance of God's will? Perhaps it is not as simple as that. For a time, Pilate struggled with the situation until he acquiesced to the wishes of the baying crowds; and that awful sound still rings in my ears.

There are fewer people here on this grim place of death away from the comfort of the city: Mary, anguished, and some friends; a temple representative to be able later to report a job nicely carried out by the Romans; of course, much soldiery, and a few 'official' mourners so infuriating and upsetting to the genuine ones.

The Pharisees have had the last laugh now, or have they? This, after all, is, I believe, what the Master predicted, though it is not at all clear to me in this haze of horror why this should be. I am not permitted to approach, and neither is Mary, his own mother. The shaft of a spear horizontally held has just told us as much. Now begins the ghastly ritual: the meticulous work of crucifixion. What words of encouragement can I shout? I cannot believe his stomach is not churning in anticipation of the further pain to come while his already broken body must be crying out in agony. I doubt I can shout at all. The Master has collapsed to the ground. The man who helped with his cross is being released from duty. The two thieves who are to be the Master's companions to the end are also on the ground, writhing. Their crosses are also being prepared: they curse and swear and make even more difficulties for themselves. A soldier kicks at them. O yes, how brave should I be? The onlookers' pain will disappear and the onlookers will shed no blood. The Master sits, head in hands at first, then with raised head. He knows what further pain his will be: the thorny crown they put on his head lends nobility, not mockery. His words about practising genuine piety spring from the sight. (In thinking about other things I can distance myself from the scene before me and escape the awful emptiness of this waiting – as empty as the hungry-faced Pharisees, fasting so faithfully.) It is easy, he has told us, to fool men into thinking something about you, but you cannot fool God. You will not impress the Father simply by what men believe about you. You can impress men with your large noisy coins dropping into the collecting box. You can even give the impression that you are filling the collecting box when you employ your skilful and practised sleight of hand. Either way, you are intent upon impressing man rather than serving God.

Is he to die for telling a few home truths?

Psalm 130

Out of the depths I cry to thee, O Lord!

Gospel

Matthew 6:1–6 and 16–18

'*Beware of practising your piety before men in order to be seen by them; for then you will have no reward from your Father who is in heaven.*

'*Thus, when you give alms, sound no trumpet before you, as the hypocrites do in the synagogues and in the streets, that they may be praised by men. Truly, I say to you, they have their reward. But when you give alms, do not let your left hand know what your right hand is doing, so that your*

*alms may be in secret; and your Father who sees in
secret will reward you.*

*'And when you pray, you must not be like the
hypocrites; for they love to stand and pray in the
synagogues and at the street corners, that they may
be seen by men. Truly, I say to you, they have their
reward. But when you pray, go into your room
and shut the door and pray to your Father who is
in secret; and your Father who sees in secret will
reward you.*

*'And when you fast, do not look dismal, like the
hypocrites, for they disfigure their faces that their
fasting may be seen by men. Truly, I say to you,
they have their reward. But when you fast, anoint
your head and wash your face, that your fasting
may not be seen by men but by your Father who is
in secret; and your Father who sees in secret will
reward you.'*

Comment

Ash Wednesday is a day of fasting at the beginning of a season of fasting. At the beginning of
his ministry, Jesus withdrew into the desert for a
period of prayer and fasting. Fasting is a spiritual
discipline through which people are prepared for
the service of God and the struggle with evil.

Fasting is not an end in itself, but a way by
which we offer up to God things – good in themselves – which can in the end enslave us if they are
put in place of God. In that offering we are made

free to know and to rejoice in the reality of God's love.

For further consideration . . .

How far do certain aspects of the Pharisees' behaviour parallel our own?

Thursday

I am now less collected but compulsively watching, watching, fascinated. My Lord is made to lie flat on the cross. A soldier orders the craftsman to begin his grisly work. But he thinks only of the work and gives meticulous attention to the preparation as he positions the arms, the hands, the legs and the feet with an unnerving, almost clinical, precision. The thieves cry out and swear again and resist, only to be again bruised into submission. My Lord is submitting without resistance to the inevitable. I do nothing; I am doing nothing; I *can* do nothing. I am watching, watching as Jesus' arms are positioned again. He is embracing the world already even before the nails secure this embrace.

I am trying to recite the prayer he taught us. It sticks on my tongue. The anticipation of the physical suffering is excruciating, and yet I cannot help but be fascinated by the scene. Now, the craftsman stands back to admire his preparation or to assess the weight of my Master – probably the latter. Should he need to position a saddle on the cross to prevent the tearing away of the body once the cross is hoisted aloft? Probably the man isn't heavy enough, the craftsman is thinking – but he looks as though he is marking the side of the cross. Perhaps he has decided to make sure. How this sickens me. Mary, in an agony of a different kind, stands here beside me, weeping and covering her eyes, and I am almost suffocated by Mary's sorrow and my sorrow, and try to concentrate on other things. Yet I am rooted here, watching, fascinated. This is true horror; waiting for even worse, knowing that it will come. The Master is already suffering much physical pain and sorrow but now smiles, albeit a difficult smile, in comfort, in the direction of his mother, who does not see.

I am sure that the Master feels alone even among these knots of people with different motives for their presence. It was alone and as a solitary figure that he faced the thoughts that tempted him in the wilderness where his mission was finally forged in the barrenness of the desert. He had to seek his Father's will and, in seeking it, the knowledge of it was made secure, the vocation clear. His course was obvious to him as soon as the obstacles were identified and other directions discarded and rejected.

Was it the Father's will that he should feed the hungry? Yes, in a sense, but he was setting us all up for heaven, not for a comfortable existence on earth. It was *our* duty as it was everyone's duty to feed the hungry, to console the dying, and to visit the sick and imprisoned. That was the natural pattern of a good life centred upon loving one's neighbour. Could he have brought everyone to the Father with even more spectacular miracles? Probably not, but can *this* really be his Father's will?

The feeding of the crowds – the five thousand or so – was that not an attempt at a humanitarian ministry? But no, I think that I realize now its significance was that of a parable concerned with sharing *him* as much as food. I don't know. These thoughts let me escape only momentarily.

Psalm

Lord, hear my voice! Let thy ears be attentive to the voice of my supplications!

Gospel

Matthew 4:1–4

Then Jesus was led up by the Spirit into the wilderness to be tempted by the devil. And he fasted forty days and forty nights, and afterward he was hungry. And the tempter came and said to him, 'If you are the Son of God, command these stones to become loaves of bread.' But he answered, 'It is written, "Man shall not live by bread alone, but by every word that proceeds from the mouth of God."'

Comment

By quoting Scripture, Jesus does not deny our real hunger but points to God as the one who alone supplies our need. In St John's Gospel, Jesus speaks of himself as the living bread, which comes down from heaven, as the bread of life. God thereby supplies our need. 'He who believes in me shall not hunger, and he who believes in me shall never thirst.'

For further consideration . . .

Do we take our Lord's words seriously? He is the 'bread of life' and also 'the way, the truth and the life'.

Friday

And here I remain watching, impassive, not intervening, frightened to remain, fearful to leave. Mary is too distraught to be comforted by a reassuring hand and my hand would reassure no one at present. My throat is tight with apprehension. Am I reassured by what is before me? Should this not reassure me, especially in the knowledge that he predicted this and much greater things? Do I understand what he did predict? He predicted our despair, sure enough.

He was tempted by the spectacular: he could certainly have achieved a spectacular ministry because he had absolute confidence that had he chosen that way he would have been protected by the angels of God, just as they have protected and secured him in the way he did choose, which means the scene I have before me. Even so, his ministry has been spectacular at times, but never spectacular for its own sake.

Over there, a beggar, one of the many odd characters who would attach themselves and who would always seem to recognize him as the Son of God. Do they now? The beggars wanted food and money (some were lazy!) but they did not expect those things of Jesus – others took care of that in his wake. That is what happened with the feeding of the crowds – spectacle was often the effect rather than the cause of his following. It was genuine modesty that appealed to him: he rejected the immodest gesture.

And lying there, his cross being marked here and there for further work, he is the epitome of modesty and selflessness. The craftsman is marking the position of his feet so that he can fix the foot rest with precision. The saddle and the foot rest will, in turn, determine the angle of the arms as they stretch up to the cross-beam. That angle will largely determine how soon the condemned man will die. If the poor creature is able to push up on his foot rest to aid his breathing for too long, or if for some reason the bodies are not permitted to remain hanging there, soldiers will break the legs, sometimes with cruel enjoyment.

Psalm

If thou, O Lord, shouldst mark iniquities, Lord, who could stand?

Gospel

Matthew 4:5–7

Then the devil took him to the holy city, and set him on the pinnacle of the temple, and said to him, 'If you are the Son of God, throw yourself down;

for it is written, "He will give his angels charge of you," and "On their hands they will bear you up, lest you strike your foot against a stone."' Jesus said to him, 'Again it is written, "You shall not tempt the Lord your God."'

Comment

Here, the devil quotes Scripture. The reply is short and to the point. Throughout the Gospels people come seeking a sign from Jesus and asking for a miracle; but miracles are ambiguous. Jesus does work miracles, but he is also very cautious about them. People seek a sign, but a sign is only given in response to faith, not to provide proof of who Jesus is.

For further consideration . . .

It is as well to remember that the devil is not shy of quoting Scripture.

Saturday

He told us that he was tempted to use his mission as the Zealots would have had him use it – with command of an army, a country, an empire, the world itself. He does not now seem to command anything but respect for his dignity in his indignity. His teaching suggested that the world had to be won for God through the heart, not by the sword.

Mary has just taken a few steps forward only to be thrust back away from her recumbent son. The soldiers wish to avoid any interference with the smooth running of the operation. I now clutch Mary's shoulder both in comfort and in order to discourage any imprudent move.

The craftsman is a wizened man in a leather apron: I have seen him about the city carrying a hide bag of the unpleasant tools of his trade. But his hammer is innocent enough: his nails blameless, cruel though both will soon become. He is making his way towards that bag of his. He kicks it open and, as he bends down, he nods to the senior soldier. The Master is pulled off the cross and to his feet and told to strip. He is now helped by two soldiers, not out of kindness but to assist in his humiliation. In the struggle with his clothes, the thorny crown is pulled off. As he stands in loin cloth only, his crown is roughly replaced with a sarcastic: 'There you are, Mr King, Sir.' The Master sways and collapses to his haunches and slumps backwards. The clothes are placed in a pile, ready for the greedy soldiers – the perks of the crucifixion fatigue party. For a moment Mary holds out a hand in the belief, I think, that the clothes might be handed to her. She now withdraws the hand knowing that that is not to be.

I have convinced myself that I am watching a drama in which I have no part and in which no part of me has any interest whatsoever. I know that this detachment will not last much longer. My great fear is that I shall pluck up what I take to be courage, and flee.

Now the craftsman selects a saddle block and a foot block from the pile not far from me and looks at me in a matter-of-fact way, seemingly in complete indifference to that which is unfolding. In doing so, though, he firmly draws me into his gruesome and evil world. Why should I resist? The Master is at this very moment the centre of it.

Psalm

But there is forgiveness with thee, that thou mayest be feared.

Gospel

Matthew 4:8–11

Again, the devil took him to a very high mountain, and showed him all the kingdoms of the world and the glory of them; and he said to him, 'All these I will give you, if you will fall down and worship me.' Then Jesus said to him, 'Begone, Satan! for it is written, "You shall worship the Lord your God and him only shall you serve."' Then the devil left him, and behold, angels came and ministered to him.

Comment

Jesus is offered all the kingdoms of the world, but at a price; and the price is surrender to the fallen world and the power of evil. The devil claims possession of the world, but of course the world is God's although it is a fallen world under the domination of evil. The lie that the world belongs to the power of evil and not to God is paralleled by the invitation to Jesus to bow down and worship the devil. Jesus counters with the clear statement that worship belongs to God alone. What and who is ultimate? Who is worthy of worship? Is it the power of evil or God the creator?

For further consideration . . .

How far does our demeanour help support the
proposition that the world is under the domination
of evil?

Lent 1

COLT
SWITCH
BRANCH

BLESSED IS HE
THAT COMETH IN
THE NAME OF
THE LORD

Monday 1

A Temple Official:

This really is most satisfactory – a happy completion indeed.

For so long we have wondered what to do for the best. A number of times the temple guards have been used to arrest him in the past, on some pretext or other, but have failed. It was just as well; the people would probably have rioted. They were besotted. But he was an infernal nuisance, disturbing the tranquillity of the cities, villages and towns. Much of his preaching was blasphemous at worst, and, at best, most disrespectful to those who so avidly carry out the will of the law. For blasphemy we were prepared to stone him – that would have been an end to him all right. But, again, the people – many times we tried to entrap him to this end. Clever, I'll give him that.

There he is now, soon to be nailed down once and for all and out of our hair for ever. He spoke lightly of his own religion, the faith of our father Abraham, but it was convenient to convert his blasphemy to treason and so win the justice of Rome.

What presumption – most fortunate for us – encouraging the crowds to blaspheme and hail

him king when he came into Jerusalem the other
day stupidly sitting on that equally stupid animal,
looking the fool he is.

Psalm

I wait for the Lord, my soul waits, and in his word
I hope.

Gospel

John 10:30, 31, 39
Matthew 21:1–3

'I and the Father are one.'

*The Jews took up stones again to stone him.
Again they tried to arrest him, but he escaped
from their hands.*

*And when they drew near to Jerusalem and
came to Bethphage, to the Mount of Olives, then
Jesus sent two disciples, saying to them, 'Go into
the village opposite you, and immediately you will
find an ass tied, and a colt with her; untie them
and bring them to me. If any one says anything to
you, you shall say, "The Lord has need of them,"
and he will send them immediately.'*

Comment

Jesus' journey to Jerusalem, his coming to the
Holy City, is seen as more than just the journey of

any Galilean countryman to the big city, and even as more than the pilgrim coming to worship and offer sacrifice at the temple. It is a new exodus, a journey of deliverance and of salvation. St John's Gospel sees it as the journey of the Son to the Father – a journey which is made by the Son's perfect response to his Father's will.

For further consideration . . .

With resolution our Lord set his face towards Jerusalem and all that that would mean. How easy is it for us to praise with our tongues one moment; to curse, the next?

Tuesday 1

The Beloved Disciple:

And now the saddle and foot rest will be secured. But there will be no rest until he breathes his last. I am trying to avoid watching Jesus: in contrast, his mother now stares at him in tearful disbelief at what we are witnessing.

The craftsman is kneeling beside the trunk of the cross and sits the saddle upon it, lining it up with the marks drawn on the side. One heavy blow from the hammer wielded by this rather slight but deceptively strong individual will fix the foot-long split nail into the wood; a second, and the nail will penetrate the saddle and pierce the main beam; a third, and the nail will be home. The split ends will be bent their separate ways after the cross has been hoisted high on the hill.

Mary and I are permitted quiet words of comfort but they would be drowned among the cries and curses of the two to be crucified with Jesus. What quiet words of comfort can you give? I can think of none even if I could articulate any. The mostly fickle crowds have dissolved: there are few of us silent on this hillside. A contrast indeed with the adulation with which he was received astride the donkey. This deeply significant gesture, as I thought at the time, now has no meaning at all.

Psalm

My soul waits for the Lord more than watchmen for the morning.

Gospel

Luke 19:32–40

So those who were sent went away and found it as he had told them. And as they were untying the colt, its owners said to them, 'Why are you untying the colt?' And they said, 'The Lord has need of it.' And they brought it to Jesus, and throwing their garments on the colt they set Jesus upon it. And as he rode along, they spread their garments on the road. As he was now drawing near, at the descent of the Mount of Olives, the whole multitude of the disciples began to rejoice and praise God with a loud voice for all the mighty works that they had seen, saying, 'Blessed is the King who comes in the name of the Lord! Peace in heaven and glory in the highest!' And some of the Pharisees in the multitude said to him, 'Teacher, rebuke your disciples.' He answered, 'I tell you, if these were silent, the very stones would cry out.'

Comment

Some of the Pharisees had heard the cries: 'Blessed is the King who comes in the name of the Lord! Peace in heaven and glory in the highest!' It was very dangerous; not at all orthodox. And they had protested about it. And so the scene was set.

For further consideration . . .

Perhaps we might compare the cry of the crowds: 'Peace in heaven and glory in the highest!' with the angel's cry of 'Glory to God in the highest, and on earth peace among men . . . !'

Wednesday 1

Yes, the crowds were full of enthusiasm and excitement on that day. Many in those crowds heard his trial: some sidled off; others cried out for Barabbas and for the blood of Jesus simply because of the prompting of the staff of the chief priests, and the elders. Most, therefore, deserted him as indeed he knew would happen. Even of the twelve, few remained and fewer remain anywhere near now. I am here not through courage. I long to run away and hide. I cannot count myself anyone's superior for my presence here.

The children always knew. 'Become like these,' he would say, 'because their instincts have not been blunted either by superstition or sophistication. They may not have years of learning but their perception is sharp.' But *what* did the children know?

The wiry old craftsman is picking up his hammer, a hammer long familiar to his hand, and so he urges me out of reverie. Three hammer blows snap mockingly at me with pent-up aggression. 'Colt! Switch! Branch!' they seem to say. The saddle on the cross is fixed.

Psalm

O Israel, hope in the Lord! For with the Lord
there is steadfast love, and with him is plenteous
redemption.

Gospel
Matthew 21:10–16

*And when he entered Jerusalem, all the city was
stirred, saying, 'Who is this?' And the crowds
said, 'This is the prophet Jesus from Nazareth of
Galilee.'*

*And Jesus entered the temple of God and drove
out all who sold and bought in the temple, and
he overturned the tables of the money-changers
and the seats of those who sold pigeons. He
said to them, 'It is written, "My house shall be
called a house of prayer"; but you make it a den of
robbers.'*

*And the blind and the lame came to him in the
temple, and he healed them. But when the chief
priests and the scribes saw the wonderful things
that he did, and the children crying out in the
temple, 'Hosanna to the Son of David!' they were
indignant; and they said to him, 'Do you hear
what these are saying?' And Jesus said to them,
'Yes; have you never read, "out of the mouth of
babes and sucklings thou hast brought perfect
praise"?'*

Comment

The prophets of Israel were often uncomfortable people. They were disturbers, prickers of the balloon of complacency. Jeremiah inveighs against those who parrot the cry 'The Temple of the Lord, The Temple of the Lord', believing themselves inviolable. Jeremiah is commanded by God to stand outside the gate of the temple and proclaim: 'The Lord, the God of Israel says this: "Amend your behaviour and your actions and I will stay with you in this place . . . but steal, would you, murder, commit adultery, perjure yourselves . . . follow alien gods? You do all this and then present yourselves in the Temple, saying 'now we are safe'. Do you take this Temple that bears my name for a robbers' den? I am not blind." '

Jesus enters the temple and drives out the traders and the sellers of sacrificial animals; the words of Jeremiah rise to his lips: '. . . but you make it a den of robbers'.

What really brought about Jesus' crucifixion? Much of it was Jesus' words and deeds about the temple.

For further consideration . . .

We are temples of the Holy Spirit. In and from these temples, we cheat, deceive and corrupt. Our Lord said that we must become as children. A monastic principle states: 'Rather feel compunction than know the meaning of the word.'

Thursday 1

And those mocking sounds warn of more vicious sounds to come. The inevitability of his crucifixion now is hammered home. Mary is clutching my arm as the craftsman moves to work on the other two crosses.

There is a little commotion. More temple officials are arriving, arguing, it seems, with a centurion. I cannot hear, but I still hear the words of the hammer. I see again the colt trotting dutifully beside my Master mounted on the ass; I see the switches torn from the trees by the people lauding their great teacher, come from God; I see again the branches torn down and spread before him to honour him on his way. I see the switch he used to drive out the deceivers and fraudsters from the temple court and I hear him weep over the temple and over Jerusalem for the inhabitants' lack of faith and lack of preparation for their own souls, despite all the prophets' warnings. I envisage the switches and branches surely used to scourge the Master before his journey here to Golgotha.

Psalm

And he will redeem Israel from all his iniquities.

Gospel

Luke 19:41–4, 47, 48

And when he drew near and saw the city he wept over it, saying, 'Would that even today you knew the things that make for peace! But now they are hid from your eyes. For the days shall come upon you, when your enemies will cast up a bank about you and surround you, and hem you in on every side, and dash you to the ground, you and your children within you, and they will not leave one stone upon another in you; because you did not know the time of your visitation.'

And he was teaching daily in the temple. The chief priests and the scribes and the principal men of the people sought to destroy him; but they did not find anything they could do, for all the people hung upon his words.

Comment

And as he comes to the crest of the Mount of Olives and sees Jerusalem, he breaks into tears. The city of peace has not known and lived by the things that belong to its peace, and embody its peace. And so judgement will come. There will not be one stone left standing on another. And so, Jesus weeps over Jerusalem; weeps over the city of peace, which has been blind to what peace is. The new Jerusalem embodies, in the power of the Resurrection, the things that belong to peace.

For further consideration . . .

We are already made new in Christ. Do we make it apparent?

Friday 1

The waiting and the watching are difficult to bear. The soldiers are deciding who should own my Master's clothes. There is much carefree fun and jollity. It is no concern of theirs that a grave miscarriage of justice is about to occur: they have seen it all before. Jesus waits.

Many in the crowds who greeted him with palms and olive branches were there because of Lazarus, the brother of Martha and Mary. He is fond of the whole family and it was for them that this extraordinary miracle was performed. Jairus' daughter he brought back to life, and that widow's son, I remember, but they were essentially domestic affairs. The raising up of Lazarus was more remarkable because it was public and seemed pregnant with meaning, just as though it were one of his parables. But that meaning is too well hidden.

It is uncomfortable to think of these things as the Master is being so carefully prepared for death.

Psalm 22

My God, my God, why hast thou forsaken me? Why art thou so far from helping me, from the words of my groaning?

Gospel

John 12:9–11, 13–16, 19

When the great crowd of the Jews learned that he was there, they came, not only on account of Jesus but also to see Lazarus, whom he had raised from the dead. So the chief priests planned to put Lazarus also to death, because on account of him many of the Jews were going away and believing in Jesus.

So they took branches of palm trees and went out to meet him, crying, Hosanna! Blessed is he who comes in the name of the Lord, even the King of Israel! And Jesus found a young ass and sat upon it; as it is written, 'Fear not, daughter of Zion; behold, your king is coming, sitting on an ass's colt!' His disciples did not understand this, at first; but when Jesus was glorified, then they remembered that this had been written of him and had been done to him.

The Pharisees then said to one another, 'You see that you can do nothing; look, the world has gone after him.'

Comment

Pilgrims, trudging up the hill to Jerusalem for the feast of the Passover, would have been stirred by the knot of Galileans around a man on a donkey. People were shouting and cheering, waving branches of palm and olive. They were cheering the man on the donkey – a very ordinary sight in itself – as though he were a king, throwing their cloaks before him as a sign of homage. A few might have thought of the prophecy of Zechariah about God's anointed one coming to the Holy City without any sign or rank of splendour. What might this mean, this symbolic coming of Jesus to Jerusalem at the time of the feast of deliverance, the celebration of the freeing of the people of Israel from slavery in Egypt?

For further consideration . . .

Lazarus was brought back to life: he would die again. Christ rose from the dead to die no more; death would have no more dominion over him.

Saturday 1

The methodical craftsman is returning to the cross in front of me. His matter-of-factness is frightening: he would have the same attitude and demeanour if he were repairing the door of my home.

The recently arrived officials from the temple are most heated in their argument with the centurion. He is holding what looks like an indictment plaque. I am ashamed to feel grateful for the diversion as I stand and wait with Mary.

I can now see others only just familiar to me by sight, and some close followers of Jesus, appearing at various distances from this point – little clutches of deep sorrow and huddles of despair. Greater numbers are watching the fate of the other prisoners. Mary and I shall be permitted to converse with Jesus once this ghastly preparation is over and the final stage reached. The death of the Christ is contrary to what I have understood. He was unwavering in asserting his special relationship to God the almighty Father, so that he is the Christ I cannot doubt. Yet how can this suffering and death be part of God's plan? What else, though, could his vineyard story foretell?

Psalm

O my God, I cry by day, but thou dost not answer;
and by night, but find no rest.

Gospel

Luke 20:1, 2, 9–16, 19

*One day, as he was teaching the people in the
temple and preaching the gospel, the chief priests
and the scribes with the elders came up and said to
him, 'Tell us by what authority you do these
things, or who it is that gave you this authority.'*

*And he began to tell the people this parable: 'A
man planted a vineyard, and let it out to tenants,
and went into another country for a long while.
When the time came, he sent a servant to the tenants, that they should give him some of the fruit of
the vineyard; but the tenants beat him, and sent
him away empty-handed. And he sent another servant; him also they beat and treated shamefully,
and sent him away empty-handed. And he sent yet
a third; this one they wounded and cast out. Then
the owner of the vineyard said, "What should I
do? I will send my beloved son; it may be that they
will respect him." But when the tenants saw him,
they said to themselves, "This is the heir; let us kill
him, that the inheritance may be ours." And they
cast him out of the vineyard and killed him. What
then will the owner of the vineyard do to them? He*

will come and destroy those tenants, and give the vineyard to others.' When they heard this, they said, 'God forbid!'

The scribes and the chief priests tried to lay hands on him at that very hour, but they feared the people; for they perceived that he had told this parable against them.

Comment

What had been proclaimed in Galilee must also be proclaimed in Jerusalem, at the very centre of the faith of Israel. Jesus rides into Jerusalem: the crowds cheer; and then? Some great intervention by God? No, but an attack on the temple traders, and an assertion about the nature of worship. No great popular rising; no expulsion of the Roman power; only, for the rest of his days in Jerusalem, the steady, inexorable, closing in of the hostile powers.

For further consideration . . .

When the hostile powers close in on the heir to the vineyard, they will kill the heir. The paradox is that the heir is also the vine itself, and God the Father the vinedresser.

Lent 2

TAKE
BREAK
FEED

Monday 2

Simon Peter:

What weakness! What shame! 'I am a worm,' as the psalmist says, 'and no man.' It was I who pronounced him the Christ: I who saw it and said so.

'Curb your exuberance,' he has said on many occasions, gently, if I became excited at the prospect of a fresh project, a new mission. Now he prepares to die as I skulk, mortified. It all began to fall apart for me in that upper room we hired. First, I would not have my feet washed, then I changed my mind: 'Wash my head and my hands as well!' I said. I felt stupid when Jesus told me that it wasn't necessary. Waves of shame alternating with self-pity wash over me now. 'I'll go to the ends of the earth for you!' I afterwards declared. 'You'll deny me, Peter, three times before cock crow.' How crushing was that condemnation! I couldn't understand these words. Why should Jesus turn on me in that way and, being forewarned, why could I not summon the strength to resist the coward's way? I was too ashamed to admit my association with him to a mere girl, who, after all, was only making a sensible observation. Three times I denied knowing Jesus, whom

I identified as the Christ. Never before has a morning alarm awakened me to the horror of my weaknesses. O, that *look* . . .

Psalm

Yet thou art holy, enthroned on the praises of Israel.

Gospel

Luke 22:1–13

Now the feast of Unleavened Bread drew near, which is called the Passover. And the chief priests and the scribes were seeking how to put him to death; for they feared the people.

Then Satan entered into Judas called Iscariot, who was of the number of the twelve; he went away and conferred with the chief priests and captains how he might betray him to them. And they were glad, and engaged to give him money. So he agreed, and sought an opportunity to betray him to them in the absence of the multitude.

Then came the day of Unleavened Bread, on which the passover lamb had to be sacrificed. So Jesus sent Peter and John, saying, 'Go and prepare the passover for us that we may eat it.' They said to him, 'Where will you have us prepare it?' He said to them, 'Behold, when you have entered the city, a man carrying a jar of water will meet you;

*follow him into the house which he enters, and tell
the householder, "The Teacher says to you, Where
is the guest room, where I am to eat the passover
with my disciples?" And he will show you a large
upper room, furnished; there make ready.' And
they went, and found it as he had told them; and
they prepared the passover.*

Comment

What is certain is that the context of Jesus' dying
was Passover; and Passover was concerned with
God's mighty acts; concerned with a deliverance
from slavery, and a remembrance of such a deliverance. The Passover was a memorial of deliverance
from Egypt. In making and keeping this memorial,
time was telescoped.

Bitter herbs were chewed so that the tasting of
bitterness linked the present with the past.

For further consideration . . .

Our 'Peterness' is very apparent. We can prepare
the upper room in the morning and deny Christ in
the evening.

Tuesday 2

The Beloved Disciple:

My arm surrounds Mary's shoulders. They shudder involuntarily now and again. We are both watching the craftsman in the foreground, perhaps as intently as a pair of apprentices watch their employer for fear of being asked searching questions they find themselves unable to answer. In the background is Jesus, naked save for a loin cloth, seemingly studying the same scene from a rather different perspective. Can he detach himself from reality and remember the tools he knew so well in his father's workshop? The calculated monotony of this lingering prelude is unbearable.

The foot block or rest has been selected – I believe it is also called a 'shoe' and there's some irony in that. In placing it on the main beam, the craftsman lines it up with the mark he has made. He now picks up one of his formidable nails – its brothers will have to perform the more bloody duties – and stands it on the block. The resounding blows quite distinctly say: 'Take! Break! Feed!' and the block is secure.

Why do those words snap at me now; those words so gently spoken? Perhaps because this violence about to erupt before me must first occur in order to make sense of his words. But what sense will it make? What sense can it make? 'Take! Break! Feed!'

Psalm

In thee our fathers trusted; they trusted, and thou didst deliver them.

Gospel

Luke 22:14–19

And when the hour came, he sat at table, and the apostles with him. And he said to them, 'I have earnestly desired to eat this passover with you before I suffer; for I tell you I shall not eat it until it is fulfilled in the kingdom of God.' And he took a cup, and when he had given thanks he said, 'Take this, and divide it among yourselves; for I tell you that from now on I shall not drink of the fruit of the vine until the kingdom of God comes.' And he took bread, and when he had given thanks he broke it and gave it to them, saying, 'This is my body which is given for you. Do this in remembrance of me.'

Comment

What is new in Jesus' action is not the taking of
bread and the giving thanks over it, but the identi-
fication of it with his body. Jesus, the host, takes
bread – bread, which is life and the most ordinary
of things, the food we need in order to live. This
very bread is my body, he says. In the Old Testament not only words but actions are prophetic. A
cloak is torn, and a kingdom is divided. Prophets
speak by signs, and these signs are seen as in some
way triggering an action which follows from
them. Jesus takes bread and breaks it, and identi-
fies it with himself. Already in the upper room, the
movement of his self-offering is begun.

For further consideration . . .

The sound of the breaking of the host on the altar
also causes the telescoping of time. However, this
food is given for our sustenance now.

Wednesday 2

The Master's body is soon to be broken on the cross rather as the bread he broke before us and called his body, but my mind can take this proposition no further. In a way, that meal had every feature and sign of being our final act together – a farewell from the Master. How could that black-hearted companion of ours precipitate this disaster?

The shoes are about to be fitted on the thieves' crosses: the thieves are a little quieter. They, like the Master, are undressed. They stole: their clothes are taken and their lives will be taken. If there is justice in their case, there is little in my Master's.

The heated discussion is subsiding: the centurion is patting the plaque and shrugging his shoulder, perhaps in sympathy with their point of view.

Difficult also to grasp were his subsequent words. The wine cup was to be as his blood, he said, poured out for all. So much I feel this a dream, that I am sure I can walk over to him, brushing through the fence of horizontal spears, and question him as to the meaning of these things. The wisdom of not doing so is borne in on me: the weapons are real; the soldiers are real; the drama no dream; the drama no make-believe.

Psalm

To thee they cried, and were saved; in thee they trusted, and were not disappointed.

Gospel

Luke 22:20–3

And likewise the cup after supper, saying, 'This cup which is poured out for you is the new covenant in my blood. But behold the hand of him who betrays me is with me on the table. For the Son of man goes as it has been determined; but woe to that man by whom he is betrayed!' And they began to question one another, which of them it was that would do this.

Comment

The bread that is broken is the bread of which Jesus said, 'This is my body.' The sign of broken bread points inexorably to the broken body and the pouring out of his blood. 'Breaking' is the language of sacrifice and sacrifice is at the heart of what was done on Calvary. At its heart it is an offering, and an immolation, for the establishment or renewal of communion. What begins in the earlier strands of the Old Testament as the offering of lambs, or the blood of bulls and goats, moves on, through the psalmist's 'the sacrifice of God is ... a broken and contrite heart ...', to an offering in which the devout man personally participates.

For further consideration ...

The outpouring of the chalice of consecrated wine is the generous spilling of the life-giving blood of the Church, as the outpouring of wine from the water pitchers in Cana is a foretaste of this Passion, established at the beginning of our Lord's ministry.

Thursday 2

More people are arriving: they are keeping their distance. Mary and I are here close to what is happening. We can move no closer. We were together at Cana when Jesus said to his mother with a smile: 'What am I to do with you? I had not intended to begin my mission on this day in this place!' He acquiesced to her entreaty and helped recover the reputation of the host. So many of his miracles were also parables: he taught us through them. And now I suddenly see that this so very domestic miracle at the beginning of his ministry showed us the outpouring of his blood on this day, which outpouring we shall soon witness.

This revelation has helped me little. Memories are rushing headlong into my mind, uncontrolled. How perverse, I am compelled to concentrate on what is happening about me in this place.

The saddles and shoes of the thieves' crosses are fixed, and indeed the indictment plaques are now being nailed. The centurion is handing another to the craftsman: I believe it to be the Master's. What does it say? Treason? Blasphemy?

If either, his words were obviously never heard.

Psalm

But I am a worm, and no man; scorned by men, and despised by the people.

Gospel

John 13:2–11

And during supper, when the devil had already put it into the heart of Judas Iscariot, Simon's son, to betray him, Jesus, knowing that the Father had given all things into his hands, and that he had come from God and was going to God, rose from supper, laid aside his garments, and girded himself with a towel. Then he poured water into a basin, and began to wash the disciples' feet and to wipe them with the towel with which he was girded. He came to Simon Peter; and Peter said to him, 'Lord, do you wash my feet?' Jesus answered him, 'What I am doing you do not know now, but afterward you will understand.' Peter said to him, 'You shall never wash my feet.' Jesus answered him, 'If I do not wash you, you have no part in me.' Simon Peter said to him, 'Lord, not my feet only but also my hands and my head!' Jesus said to him, 'He who has bathed does not need to wash, except for his feet, but he is clean all over; and you are clean, but not all of you.' For he knew who was to betray him; that was why he said, 'You are not all clean.'

Comment

The breaking of the Lord's body on the cross was preceded by another breaking, a breaking of communion by betrayal. Our Lord's sacrifice was born of the darkness of betrayal and abandonment. With the cross he bears the weight of sin, the weight of betrayal, the weight of the denial of communion.

For further consideration . . .

As the host is broken upon the altar as a prelude to Communion, how often has our betrayal of his Word broken that very Communion?

Friday 2

Jesus told me who he knew would betray him to the chief priests. In remorse, Judas has, I hear, killed himself. 'This is the man, the man I am greeting. This is he.' What did he hope to gain? Possibly a little money? But many liars and perjurers were found or paid in order to enable the chief priests to take Jesus before Pilate. If the Romans kill him, the chief priests will not be blamed by the people. Judas, then, merely identified Jesus in the darkness – the first step in the chief priests' plan to be rid of the Christ because he did not fit their preconception of the Saviour. He frightened them.

But the sad sight before me now, wept over by his mother, will frighten few people. He now suffers extreme degradation and humiliation. Did he not explain all this to us? Could he have meant condemnation as a state criminal and death in this way? This does not fit my preconception of the Christ either.

The craftsman is reading the plaque he has been given. He looks surprised and looks up at the centurion who once more shrugs his shoulders and turns the palms of his hands upwards in a gesture of mock hopelessness.

Psalm

All who see me mock at me, they make mouths at me.

Gospel

John 12:21b–27

'Truly, truly, I say to you, one of you will betray me.' The disciples looked at one another, uncertain of whom he spoke. One of his disciples, whom Jesus loved, was lying close to the breast of Jesus; so Simon Peter beckoned to him and said, 'Tell us who it is of whom he speaks.' So lying thus, close to the breast of Jesus, he said to him, 'Lord, who is it?' Jesus answered, 'It is he to whom I shall give this morsel when I have dipped it.' So when he had dipped the morsel, he gave it to Judas, the son of Simon Iscariot.

Comment

Jesus lets Judas go. The betrayer is free to choose what to do and how to act. Judas shows his failure to recognize the demands of love by choosing the darkness rather than the light.

For further consideration . . .

Our betrayals are often rather subtler than Judas'.
They are often difficult to detect as we keep them
from ourselves.

Saturday 2

Jesus told Peter that he could not follow him now but that he would do so later. Is *this* his route back to the Father? What of us now? Shall we fish again and, in time, put aside these years in our minds as nothing more than an interesting interlude? I cannot believe that it is all to no avail. For Jesus, each event has always seemed a step forward, whether a modest triumph or an acrimonious rejection.

Paradoxically, I have begun almost to like the grotesque little craftsman and to dissociate him from his grisly work, and in so doing a feeling of disloyalty floods over me. However, I know that he is the last person the Master would condemn.

I think I can see the other Marys and Salome keeping to themselves at a distance. It would be of comfort to me and to his mother if they were to join us because worse is to come and Mary's despair will deepen further as the hours die.

Psalm

They wag their heads; 'He committed his cause to the Lord; let him deliver him, let him rescue him, for he delights in him!'

Gospel

John 13:12–17, 34–8

When he had washed their feet, and taken his garments, and resumed his place, he said to them, 'Do you know what I have done to you? You call me Teacher and Lord; and you are right, for so I am. If I then, your Lord and Teacher, have washed your feet, you also ought to wash one another's feet. For I have given you an example, that you also should do as I have done to you. Truly, truly, I say to you, a servant is not greater than his master; nor is he who is sent greater than he who sent him. If you know these things, blessed are you if you do them.

'A new commandment I give to you, that you love one another; even as I have loved you, that you also love one another. By this all men will know that you are my disciples, if you have love for one another.'

Simon Peter said to him, 'Lord, where are you going?' Jesus answered, 'Where I am going you cannot follow me now; but you shall follow afterward.' Peter said to him, 'Lord, why cannot I follow you now? I will lay down my life for you.' Jesus answered, 'Will you lay down your life for me? Truly, truly, I say to you, the cock will not crow, till you have denied me three times.'

Comment

The betrayer has gone, and Jesus speaks to his
disciples. The problem of keeping command-
ments, as St Paul found and argues in his letter to
the Romans, is that commands are double-edged.
We fail, and the law we believed we could obey,
and which we strove to follow, stands in judgement over our failure. However, Paul made the
overwhelming discovery that God had already
accepted him in love by the very act of the sending
of his Son into the world.

For further consideration . . .

Despite our betrayals and denials we are accepted
in love by God.

Lent 3

Sweat
Blood
Kiss

Monday 3

Mary, the Mother of Jesus:

O Heavenly Father, you are about to take away the son you gave me all those years ago. Your messenger told me that his name would be great and that he would be the one spoken of by the prophets of old. With Joseph, I found a place in Bethlehem and there I suckled him. The common men came from the hilltop and illustrious ones knelt before him. We named him and presented him to you. Through Simeon you told me of momentous things that would occur because of him and that I should suffer in my duties to you. These warnings have come horribly to pass. Forgive me. Hold him in your arms until he commends his spirit to you. Give me strength and steadfastness, perseverance and resolution to remain here and faithful to my son and your son, until and beyond the time you take him to continue to do your will. I believe but do not understand. Strengthen me also to be able to do what you would have me do. Thank you, O Heavenly Father, for the gift of your son, of my son; for the work he has done and for the work he will do.

Psalm

Yet thou art he who took me from the womb;
thou didst keep me safe upon my mother's breasts.

Gospel

Mark 14:32–8

*And they went to a place which was called
Gethsemane; and he said to his disciples, 'Sit here,
while I pray.' And he took with him Peter and
James and John, and began to be greatly distressed
and troubled. And he said to them, 'My soul is
very sorrowful, even to death; remain here, and
watch.' And going a little farther, he fell on the
ground and prayed that, if it were possible, the
hour might pass from him. And he said, 'Abba,
Father, all things are possible to thee; remove this
cup from me; yet not what I will, but what thou
wilt.' And he came and found them sleeping, and
he said to Peter, 'Simon, are you asleep? Could
you not watch one hour? Watch and pray that you
may not enter into temptation; the spirit indeed is
willing, but the flesh is weak.'*

Comment

Jesus existed as one of us, in our situation, living
as man towards death, living as man with the
possibility of God. In his life the power and pre-

sence of God were so manifest that in encountering him men and women were made whole, knew themselves judged and knew themselves forgiven. 'Lord, to whom else shall we go?' said Peter. 'You have the words of eternal life.'

For further consideration . . .

If to the God of Love we are open about our weaknesses and sin, we then know forgiveness.

Tuesday 3

The Beloved Disciple:

Soon the cross will be hauled to a position where it can be hoisted into its shuttered slot in the ground. But first, the indictment plaque will be fixed. The order of these things is meticulous and well rehearsed.

A smaller nail has been selected and, at what will be the uppermost part of the cross, the wizened man is now kneeling with hammer held. Three hammer blows secure the plaque, and again, three single syllables now assail my ears. The last seems to hiss as the hammer – its job done – ricochets off the plaque. 'Sweat! Blood! Kiss!'

I am looking at Jesus slumped against a tussock, waiting to be taken to the cross and fixed to it. I cannot see the indictment from this angle. I can see a rivulet of startlingly red blood from the point of a thorn in the middle of his forehead making its way down his nose. That was the path taken by great drops of sweat in Gethsemane as Jesus, deep in prayer, wrestled with what he knew was to come.

Psalm

Upon thee was I cast from my birth, and since my mother bore me thou hast been my God.

Gospel

Luke 22:43–6

And there appeared to him an angel from heaven, strengthening him. And being in an agony he prayed more earnestly; and his sweat became like great drops of blood falling down upon the ground. And when he rose from prayer, he came to the disciples and found them sleeping for sorrow, and he said to them, 'Why do you sleep? Rise and pray that you may not enter into temptation.'

Comment

'You have the words of eternal life,' said Peter. And yet Jesus, so powerfully attractive and at the same time so challenging, spoke of the necessity for us to find that true life through a dying. It is the man who is willing to lose his life who will find it, whereas he who takes care to save his life will lose it. Jesus' disciples must take up their cross and follow him. They are to be baptized with the baptism that he is baptized with and drink the same cup – that cup which Jesus in agony, grappling with the dust of Gethsemane and sweating blood, longed to pass from him.

For further consideration . . .

If we let our cross drop, it will fall again across the shoulders of Christ himself.

Wednesday 3

His head glistened as though anointed with the oil produced by the presses there at Gethsemane. We all believed him chosen, anointed for God's purposes. The scene before me is despair and defeat but the Master's attitude there in the garden was of one reaching the final stages of his life's work, painful and gruelling though it was going to be. His followers certainly did not support him in this belief. Slowly they fell away during the succeeding events. In the garden vigil we could scarcely keep our eyes open. We did not grasp the importance or the significance of the occasion. He knew, of course. But the evidence of this scene before me looks little like victory and achievement. God, our Father in heaven, give me understanding.

The craftsman is standing back from the crosses as they are dragged further over so that the bases will point to the underground scabbards that will hold them upright.

Psalm

Be not far from me, for trouble is near and there is none to help.

Gospel

Matthew 23:42–5

Again, for the second time, he went away and prayed, 'My Father, if this cannot pass unless I drink it, thy will be done.' And again he came and found them sleeping, for their eyes were heavy. So, leaving them again, he went away and prayed for the third time, saying the same words. Then he came to the disciples and said to them, 'Are you still sleeping and taking your rest? Behold, the hour is at hand, and the Son of man is betrayed into the hands of sinners.'

Comment

Jesus shows us that there is a dying to be accomplished before we come to the moment of his earthly death, a dying that is a dying to self, a dying to sin, to that placing of ourselves at the centre of our universe of meaning.

For further consideration . . .

There are many things that militate against our fulfilling our vocations as 'other Christs'. Why does not Christ's love shine from my face?

Thursday 3

Judas appeared, in the company of thugs and agents of the chief priests and elders, to greet Jesus and to point him out to the mob. It was dark and there were few lanterns and torches. Even then, Jesus appeared master of the situation. 'There's no need for all this. I am here.'

He now no longer appears master of the situation – unless all these people are doing what God requires of them. If this is so, it is beyond my comprehension. It is all too vile. The Judas kiss marked him out to die.

The Master is calm, knowing that he will soon be taken to the cross once more; but the thieves are not. The rising crescendo of swearing and cursing as they realize their time approaches accompanies the grunts of the soldiers as they draw the crosses along the ground to the places allotted.

Psalm

Many bulls encompass me, strong bulls of Bashan surround me.

Gospel

Matthew 26:46–50

'Rise, let us be going; see, my betrayer is at hand.'

While he was still speaking, Judas came, one of the twelve, and with him a great crowd with swords and clubs, from the chief priests and the elders of the people. Now the betrayer had given them a sign, saying, 'The one I shall kiss is the man; seize him.' And he came up to Jesus at once and said, 'Hail, Master!' And he kissed him. Jesus said to him, 'Friend, why are you here?' Then they came up and laid hands on Jesus and seized him.

Comment

Let us remind ourselves that the breaking of the Lord's body on the cross was preceded by another breaking, a breaking of communion by the darkness of betrayal. The kiss of Judas is part of the Passion of our Lord; the betrayal by 'my own familiar friend whom I trusted, who has lifted up his hand against me'.

For further consideration . . .

In pointing out the Master in the darkness, Judas is denying his association with him. 'This is the man all right: don't, however, associate me with him.' Can these be our words?

Friday 3

There is a level 'table' here on the top of the hill, so that any final adjustments can be made by the craftsman of the day and the crosses completed for the work they will have to do. They are then positioned correctly, ready for the fixing of the prisoners. In popular idiom they are then 'launched'. It appears that the Master will be flanked by the two miscreants.

Mary is bracing herself for the cruel wounding of her son's hands and feet, which will test us all.

That Jesus healed the injured servant's ear passed almost unnoticed at his arrest. In fact, he facilitated his own arrest by quelling the scuffles that had broken out around him, thus making it easier for the officers of the temple to apprehend him.

All three crosses are in position and the cross on the right will be occupied first. A soldier struggles with one of the thieves and lays him flat on the cross. Suddenly, the man is releasing a blood-curdling yell.

Psalm

They open wide their mouths at me, like a ravening and roaring lion.

Gospel

Luke 22:48–51

But Jesus said to him, 'Judas, would you betray the Son of man with a kiss?' And when those who were about him saw what would follow, they said, 'Lord, shall we strike with the sword?' And one of them stuck the slave of the high priest and cut off his right ear. But Jesus said, 'No more of this!' And he touched his ear and healed him.

Comment

The Passion of our Lord begins in the darkness of betrayal and abandonment.

For further consideration . . .

With the identifying kiss, Judas has set in motion a chain of events. His later regret comes too late: the switch has been thrown.

Saturday 3

His capture was aided by the power of darkness and those who perpetrated it are retained in the clutches of that darkness.

The nails secure the thief. The Master is next. No, curiously, it has been decided to secure the other thief first and leave the central cross unoccupied for a few moments more. The other is being led over to his cross. He knows further resistance is useless. The nailing of these two fails to affect me or Mary except with a feeling of sympathy for their pain. This is merely a prelude: we are conserving our indignation.

The Master now looks up and across to his mother, then to me. He shakes his head slowly and holds up his right hand as if to say 'Keep calm, all is well.' His head and hand drop to their former positions.

The craftsman looks pleased. Now he is selecting three more large-headed nails for much crueller work.

Psalm

I am poured out like water, and all my bones are out of joint; my heart is like wax, it is melted within my breast.

Gospel

Luke 22:52–3

Then Jesus said to the chief priests and captains of the temple and elders, who had come out against him, 'Have you come out as against a robber, with swords and clubs? When I was with you day after day in the temple, you did not lay hands on me. But this is your hour, and the power of darkness.'

Comment

Jesus took bread 'on the night that he was betrayed'. The writer of the Epistle to the Hebrews sees what was done on Cavalry as the end of sacrifice, and in that sense the definitive sacrifice. And the same Epistle speaks of Christ as the Great High Priest, the end of priesthood and the end of sacrifice come together in the one who is both priest and victim, the offerer and the offered.

For further consideration . . .

Darkness is the cloak of sin. Christ illuminates the darkest recesses; that morning star who dispels the darkness and night.

Lent 4

PRIEST
KING
JUDGE

Monday 4

Pontius Pilate:

My wife sent a message during my examination of Jesus. 'Have nothing to do with the condemnation of Jesus.' Her intuition is always impeccable. However, when he was to be brought before me I was compelled to hear what the Jewish authorities had to say. I could not retort 'My wife is uneasy about all this, take the case elsewhere.' I was compelled to take the case.

I had heard about him of course: who hadn't? But what a man! He was not, though, what I expected; a philosopher, clearly, and a man with an athletic mind revealed, paradoxically, by his saying very little. 'What is truth?' I asked, because the conversation, such as it was, was difficult for me. At first, I thought 'What is truth?' to be a clever piece of rhetoric: then it dawned on me that it wasn't. There is manifestly only one truth but we make our own with borrowed facets of the real truth affixed, to beguile the opponent. There are Roman truths and Jewish truths. There is chief priests' truth; there is expedient truth; there is convenient truth; there is half-remembered truth, forgotten truth and, finally, untruth.

I took note of my wife's cautionary words.

When I discovered that the chief priests were determined the man whom they feared should die, I told them I should wash my hands of the case. 'Good,' they said. 'We are happy to have the responsibility.'

Now as he waits on Golgotha it's immaterial to him who has washed his hands of his death or who is shouldering responsibility for it. After giving in to their demands – and for the sake of expediency it was prudent that I should do so – I was powerless to do any more except enjoy the satisfaction of giving instructions for his indictment plaque. What indeed is truth?

Psalm

My strength is dried up like potsherd, and my tongue cleaves to my jaws; thou dost lay me in the dust of death.

Gospel

John 18:12–14, 19–24

So the band of soldiers and their captain and the officers seized Jesus and bound him. First they led him to Annas; for he was the father-in-law of Caiaphas, who was high priest that year. It was Caiaphas who had given counsel to the Jews that it was expedient that one man should die for the people.

The high priest then questioned Jesus about his disciples and his teaching. Jesus answered him, 'I have spoken openly to the world; I have always taught in synagogues and in the temple, where all Jews come together; I have said nothing secretly. Why do you ask me, what I said to them; they know what I said.' When he had said this, one of the officers standing by struck Jesus with his hand, saying, 'Is that how you answer the high priest?' Jesus answered him, 'If I have spoken wrongly, bear witness to the wrong, but if I have spoken rightly, why do you strike me?' Annas then sent him bound to Caiaphas the high priest.

Comment

The Jewish leaders had little liking for potential disturbers of the peace. Cruel reprisals were likely to follow if the Romans felt threatened. Not just one or two, but several hundred might be crucified to teach the others a lesson. So the high priest counsels that it is expedient that one man die for the people. What is more, Caiaphas would have the support of the Pharisees – and that was by no means always the case. These very careful religious men were known not to care for the teaching of Jesus – a dangerous radical.

For further consideration . . .

How often do we think it expedient – politic and convenient but not necessarily honest or just – for us to do or say what we do or say?

Tuesday 4

The Beloved Disciple:

So desperately did the high priest examine him on the charge of blasphemy that the examination was farcical. Many times had the same accusations been levelled against him. It was enough to hear the accusation; that was sufficient.

Mary is clasping my hand tight and I am clasping hers. We milk for courage and fortitude as the Master is led to succumb to the bloody skills of the craftsman. The craftsman is long-skilled and trained in woodwork and metalwork: he has had to acquire skill to mix his materials further and add flesh to his repertoire. The Master does not need to be pulled or pushed. He is walking the few paces. He is lowering himself and positioning himself, to the genuine admiration of the centurion. My innards now feel twisted and torn as anticipation and apprehension take effect.

Mary has freed her hand and is burying her face in both her hands and falling to her knees.

Psalm

Yea, dogs are round about me; a company of evil-doers encircle me; they have pierced my hands and feet.

Gospel

Luke 22:66–71

When day came, the assembly of the elders of the people gathered together, both chief priests and scribes; and they led him away to their council, and they said, 'If you are the Christ, tell us.' But he said to them, 'If I tell you, you will not believe; and if I ask you, you will not answer. But from now on the Son of man shall be seated at the right hand of the power of God.' And they all said, 'Are you the Son of God, then?' And he said to them, 'You say that I am.' And they said, 'What further testimony do we need? We have heard it ourselves from his own lips.'

Comment

Earlier, the Pharisees had advised Jesus on his entry into Jerusalem: 'Teacher, tell them to shut up; you know that those slogans are not only potential dynamite, they are also unorthodox; if you allow it to go on you are implying that you are the chosen King, the Messiah, God's representative.' And all that Jesus had said was that if he were to stop them cheering, the stones would start shouting. He had shown he endorsed such ideas; a dangerous character indeed.

For further consideration . . .

Jesus displays kingship and kingliness. May we reveal the nature of his kingdom in our very lives.

Wednesday 4

I now cannot turn away or hide my face. I am watching intently. A nail has been selected and is in the craftsman's hand: his hammer in the other. The left arm of Jesus has been positioned and he does not resist as the nail is rested on his hand. The soldier's knee is not required. Three hammer blows and the Master winces: 'Priest! King! Judge!' The words rush at me more terrifyingly as I know they accompany searing pain.

The chief priests pressed the high priest. The chief priests were jealous of their position, the high priest of his. Somehow the charge of blasphemy had to be converted into treason. 'Priest' whispers about my ears; 'priest' – there to protect the sacred traditions, the law, the prophets, justice; 'priest' – there to be a priest of God.

After the initial shock of the nail's penetrating her son's flesh, Mary is uncovering her face to allow its sorrow to stare at her son.

Psalm

I can count my bones – they stare and gloat over me.

Gospel

John 18:17, 18a, 25–32

The maid who kept the door said to Peter, 'Are not you also one of this man's disciples?' He said, 'I am not.' Now the servants and officers had made a charcoal fire, because it was cold. Now Simon Peter was standing and warming himself. They said to him, 'Are not you also one of his disciples?' He denied it and said, 'I am not.' One of the servants of the high priest, a kinsman of the man whose ear Peter had cut off, asked, 'Did I not see you in the garden with him?' Peter again denied it; and at once the cock crowed.

Then they led Jesus from the house of Caiaphas to the praetorium. It was early. They themselves did not enter the praetorium, so that they might not be defiled, but might eat the passover. So Pilate went out to them and said, 'What accusation do you bring against this man?' They answered him, 'If this man were not an evildoer, we would not have handed him over.' Pilate said to them, 'Take him yourselves and judge him by your own law.' The Jews said to him, 'It is not lawful for us to put any man to death.' This was to fulfil the word which Jesus had spoken to show by what death he was to die.

Comment

The pain of the betrayal by Judas must have been keen and terrible, and so too the denial of Peter – Peter who had been the first to confess his faith in Jesus as the Christ of God. Peter's assertion: 'No, I don't know him, I really don't know him. I don't know what you are talking about. How could you think I had anything to do with that man, that one on the losing side, that one who might land me on trial too if I admit I know him? Jesus? No, I never knew him.'

For further consideration . . .

When the cock began to crow, Peter felt regret. The crowing of the cock meant something to Peter only because of Jesus' prediction. The cock crow was indeed the morning alarm for Peter to come to his senses. May we be alert to this alarm.

Thursday 4

The other nails will be easier – for me, at least. To prolong the agony, the craftsman has been called to loop the ropes around the cross-beams of the other two crosses so that they can be 'launched' either side of the place reserved for the Master's cross. The Master lies gazing sadly upwards: his left arm fixed now until death.

Kingship was their masterstroke. If he claimed kingship, then the Roman authorities must be made to take an interest. In their appeal to Pilate, the chief priests were adamant that he was a threat to Caesar. What would they care?

The other Marys and Salome have drawn nearer and we have just exchanged glances but no words. Mary's sister is coming towards us. She is extending an arm to clutch Mary's arm. She now returns to the others a few paces to our right.

Psalm

They divide my garments among them, and for my raiment they cast lots.

Gospel

John 18:33–38a

Pilate entered the praetorium again and called Jesus, and said to him, 'Are you the King of the Jews?' Jesus answered, 'Do you say this of your own accord, or did others say it to you about me?' Pilate answered, 'Am I a Jew? Your own nation and the chief priests have handed you over to me; what have you done?' Jesus answered, 'My kingship is not of this world; if my kingship were of this world, my servants would fight, that I might not be handed over to the Jews; but my kingship is not from the world.' Pilate said to him, 'So you are a king?' Jesus answered, 'You say that I am a king. For this I was born, and for this I have come into the world, to bear witness to the truth. Every one who is of the truth hears my voice.' Pilate said to him, 'What is truth?'

Comment

St John sees the cross as the place of our Lord's glorification, the place where he is enthroned as a king. In St John's account of the trial before Pilate, there is a heavy irony in that it is supposed to be Jesus who is on trial.

For further consideration . . .

Only after Pilate's equivocation and Caiaphas' thoughts of expediency are nailed to the cross along with our sin will Truth be apparent.

Friday 4

Priest! King! Judge! still reverberate. All three words should suggest the comfort of justice and mercy. Now they simply mean corruption, perjury and the slaughter of the innocent.

In a few hours my life has been turned on its head. His teaching, his parables and his miracles, relating to the Kingdom of Heaven, seem meaningless. But why should they? That the servant of God, the Son of Man, the Son of God the Father, should suffer has been his constant theme and the theme of the prophets. Why should I now doubt? And yet what can now possibly come to spell victory and triumph? Lazarus comes to mind, and the parable of the vineyard, but nothing really helps.

Mary is gazing at Jesus through large, sad, tear-filled eyes. And she stands again.

Psalm

But thou, O Lord, be not far off! O thou my help hasten to my aid!

Gospel

Luke 23:4–16

And Pilate said to the chief priests and the multitudes, 'I find no crime in this man.' But they were urgent, saying, 'He stirs up the people, teaching throughout all Judea, from Galilee even to this place.'

When Pilate heard this, he asked whether the man was a Galilean. And when he learned that he belonged to Herod's jurisdiction, he sent him over to Herod, who was himself in Jerusalem at that time. When Herod saw Jesus, he was very glad, for he had long desired to see him, because he had heard about him, and he was hoping to see some sign done by him. So he questioned him at some length; but he made no answer. The chief priests and the scribes stood by, vehemently accusing him. And Herod with his soldiers treated him with contempt and mocked him; then, arraying him in gorgeous apparel, he sent him back to Pilate. And Herod and Pilate became friends with each other that very day, for before this they had been at enmity with each other.

Pilate then called together the chief priests and the rulers and the people, and said to them, 'You brought me this man as one who was perverting the people; and after examining him before you, behold, I did not find this man guilty of any of your charges against him; neither did Herod, for

he sent him back to us. Behold, nothing deserving
death has been done by him; I will therefore
chastise him and release him.'

Comment

But it is Pilate, Herod and the Jewish leaders who
are on trial, and both by silence and comment,
Jesus shows that he is the one who judges.

For further consideration . . .

Our actions and words judge us long before we
reach trial.

Saturday 4

The crosses of the thieves are successfully looped and their bases placed behind the shafts at the start of two forty-five degree slopes into the shafts. Two soldiers stand guard at the base of the right-hand cross and two soldiers hold the ropes. The centurion cries out and the cross rises creakingly and precariously upwards, jolting violently as it finds its way into the shallow shaft. It sways slightly, still held by the soldiers. One of the soldiers at the foot of the cross drops the vast wooden block behind and the cross is set. The operation has caused the unfortunate man to cry out in pain as his hands tear slightly; hands that have stolen, it is true. My Lord's hands will similarly suffer: his hands have blessed, healed and broken bread.

Psalm

Deliver my soul from the sword, my life from the power of the dog!

Gospel

Matthew 27:15–23

Now at the feast the governor was accustomed to release for the crowd any one prisoner whom they wanted. And they had then a notorious prisoner, called Barabbas. So when they had gathered, Pilate said to them, 'Whom do you want me to release for you, Barabbas or Jesus who is called Christ?' For he knew that it was out of envy that they had delivered him up. Besides, while he was sitting on the judgement seat, his wife had sent word to him, 'Have nothing to do with that righteous man, for I have suffered much over him today in a dream.' Now the chief priests and the elders persuaded the people to ask for Barabbas and destroy Jesus. The governor again said to them, 'Which of the two do you want me to release for you?' And they said, 'Barabbas.' Pilate said to them, 'Then what shall I do with Jesus who is called Christ?' They all said, 'Let him be crucified.' And he said, 'Why, what evil has he done?' But they shouted all the more, 'Let him be crucified.'

Comment

Crucifixion was the most appalling death meted out to criminals – a death which for all the Jews meant that one who suffered it was regarded as quite beyond the pale, quite apart from the community of Israel. Yet it is from this death that the Glory of God is shown. He is lifted up on the cross – the King enthroned.

For further consideration . . .

The mouths that exclaimed 'Hosanna!' now cry 'Barabbas!'

Lent 5

STRIP
SCOURGE
MOCK

Monday 5

Simon of Cyrene:

... a passer-by, an annual visitor, along with
countrymen from Cyrene, for many successive
years, an outsider, but of the Jewish faith. But
as a passer-by with my sons and, briefly, as a
bystander, I watched the sorry procession with
agitated soldiers anxious to speed along the men
with their burdens of death. The weakest stum-
bled and fell. He had already been badly bruised
by other means and on his head was a halo of
thorns – in all his pain he seemed to wear it as a
crown and in so doing gently mock the mockers.
He was extraordinary. He reached my point in the
crowd and tripped again. A soldier made a bee-
line for me: perhaps I was the tallest, the shortest,
or the darkest, it matters not. I was temporarily
conscripted to aid this man to Golgotha. My
annoyance at this peremptory treatment subsided
on even closer inspection of this man. What had
he done? I had heard rumours about him but they
were rumours about a ruler not about a criminal.
A few yards on and a woman rushed out from the
crowd to mop the man's brow. She stepped back
and looked at her handkerchief. I shifted the
weight of the base of the cross from one shoulder

to the other as best I could. I was already bruised. To encourage me, the soldier showed me his cat-o'-nine-tails.

I continued to follow the bent and crouching figure until we reached the place of execution. Did I help him? I hardly think I did. I was relieved of my temporary duty and told to go. Then, in a moment of exquisite poignancy, the poor, condemned man turned to me and thanked me.

I feel that I ought to have remained with the man to be of some comfort to him. Instead, I am returning to the city while behind me I know that duties are being performed that will lead to his death. I resolve to seek out the man's pupils. What sort of teacher was he? What was his message?

Psalm

Save me from the mouth of the lion, my afflicted soul from the horns of the wild oxen!

Gospel

Matthew 27:24–6

So when Pilate saw that he was gaining nothing, but rather that a riot was beginning, he took water and washed his hands before the crowd, saying, 'I am innocent of this righteous man's blood; see to it yourselves.' And all the people answered, 'His blood be on us and on our children!' Then he

*released for them Barabbas, and having scourged
Jesus, delivered him to be crucified.*

Comment

Pilate abdicates responsibility. Jesus is sentenced
as a criminal, taking the place of the criminal,
Barabbas. Jesus remains steadfast, living out in
perfect obedience his mission in the world. By
his steadfastness Jesus is victorious over all the
double-dealing, falsity and hypocrisy. This is the
light shining in the darkness, which darkness
could not overcome, of which John wrote at the
beginning of his Gospel.

For further consideration . . .

Can we absolve ourselves from responsibility for
our actions merely by saying so?

Tuesday 5

The Beloved Disciple:

The soldiers who are keeping us at a distance have moved a step forward to receive instructions. One is being asked to assisted with the second cross. He is slightly reluctant because his duties have not been at all strenuous so far. Instinctively, Mary and I move nearer the Master's recumbent body and I now see the emphatic words of the indictment which is no indictment at all: 'Jesus of Nazareth, King of the Jews'. It is as though Pontius Pilate is saying to Caiaphas, 'You demanded his blood; remember his blood is that of a king.' The paradox weighs heavily, and with more Roman grunts and prisoner's screams the second cross rises, sways and is now secured.

The two crosses seem to beckon the horizontal cross of Jesus with the chilling words, 'You cannot escape; your place is here with us.' And so it is: the gap between the crosses will soon be filled.

The craftsman returns to his duty.

Psalm

I will tell of thy name to my brethren; in the midst
of the congregation I will praise thee.

Gospel

John 19:10–15

*Pilate therefore said to him, 'You will not speak to
me? Do you not know that I have power to release
you, and power to crucify you?' Jesus answered
him, 'You would have no power over me unless it
had been given you from above; therefore he who
delivered me to you has the greater sin.'*

*Upon this Pilate sought to release him, but the
Jews cried out, 'If you release this man, you are
not Caesar's friend; every one who makes himself
a king, sets himself against Caesar.' When Pilate
heard these words, he brought Jesus out and sat
down on the judgement seat at a place called The
Pavement, and in Hebrew, Gabbatha. Now it was
the day of Preparation of the Passover; it was
about the sixth hour. He said to the Jews, 'Here is
your King!' They cried out, 'Away with him, away
with him, crucify him!' Pilate said to them, 'Shall
I crucify your King?' The chief priests answered,
'We have no king but Caesar.'*

Comment

Jesus is a king, though not a king in the sense that
Pilate understands. The religious leaders respond
to Pilate by urging him that the only king they
have is Caesar. And yet, St John wants us to see
that yes, indeed, here is a king. But when Pilate
earlier says, 'Behold the man', John wishes us to
hear, 'Behold *the* man' – the proper, true man, the
very pattern of what man made in the image of
God was meant to be.

For further consideration . . .

By the kiss, Judas is, in effect, saying to the mob:
'Behold the man'. Pilate presents Jesus with those
very words.

Wednesday 5

Another flat-headed nail has been selected and is being spun in the air and caught by the craftsman as if to lighten the occasion. But he is indifferent to and remote from the scene. He is kneeling to secure the second arm of the Master. Now the world's embrace is there again, about to be fixed for all time. Can this really be the terrible defeat it seems if he really did say – I am sure he did – 'Those who have seen me have seen the Father' and 'I am in the Father and Father is in me'?

Three more hammer blows: 'Strip! Scourge! Mock!' they now say and the recent horrors come again to mind. 'The King of the Jews', they tell us after they have stripped him, whipped him and mocked him. The owner of the vineyard will be angry and he will cast them out for ever. Mary stares.

Psalm

You who fear the Lord, praise him all you sons of Jacob, glorify him, and stand in awe of him, all you sons of Israel!

Gospel

Matthew 27:27–31

Then the soldiers of the governor took Jesus into the praetorium, and they gathered the whole battalion before him. And they stripped him and put a scarlet robe upon him, and plaiting a crown of thorns they put it on his head, and put a reed in his right hand. And kneeling before him they mocked him, saying, 'Hail, King of the Jews!' And they spat upon him, and took the reed and struck him on the head. And when they had mocked him, they stripped him of the robe, and put his own clothes on him, and led him away to crucify him.

Comment

Jesus is dressed in a robe – a cloak of one of the soldiers – and a painful, ludicrous crown, in mock kingship. The soldiers' games simply underline the truth of his kingship.

For further consideration . . .

In the enjoyment of another's helplessness, we reveal ours.

Thursday 5

His palms are filling with blood and he has called upon the Father to forgive his executioners. 'They don't know what they do,' he has just added. Will the Father now come, or is he here already? With one or two more nails the craftsman's job will be done. He will go away satisfied with his day's work. He will be paid well. Will he be touched by the generosity of his victim, in word and in deed? I too ask God to forgive. Do *I* forgive, though?

The soldiers, encouraged by the Jews, much enjoyed their mockery of the Master. They loved their thorny crown and that they could strike and whip a king. The temple servants enjoyed it too. 'Who hit you?' 'If you are a half-decent prophet, you could tell me my name.' Someone found a piece of scarlet cloth to make the scene even more grotesque. The prophets of old were violently rejected when they pronounced upon matters close to the heart.

The Master sighs.

Psalm

For he has not despised or abhorred the affliction of the afflicted; and he has not hid his face from him, but has heard, when he cried to him.

Gospel

Mark 15:21

And they compelled a passer-by, Simon of Cyrene, who was coming in from the country, the father of Alexander and Rufus, to carry his cross.

Comment

We are bidden to take up our cross and follow him. 'Christ leads me through no darker room than he went through before,' wrote Richard Baxter.

To share in the Easter victory is to share in a love which turns all situations of despair into hope, all places of darkness into light, the destruction of death into endless life. But the way to that victory is the way of the cross and we cannot know the life which God offers to us without entering into the meaning of the cross; without learning something of the way in which suffering can be used that is redemptive and transforming. We are baptized into the dying of Jesus. In the broken bread and poured out wine of the Eucharist we are sustained by the life and love which is at the very heart of Jesus' dying. We cannot escape from the cross as the very measure of our Christian faith and our Christian life.

For further consideration . . .

Simon takes up the Master's cross in an effort to show us our vocation.

Friday 5

In asking the Father to forgive, has Jesus also forgiven? He forgives and the Father forgives. 'The Father is in me and I in him,' he said.

Even so, these things make little sense to us – two forlorn spectators, soon to be mourners, on a hill outside Jerusalem – one a friend and disciple, the other a mother, a mother who brought him up and nurtured him and stayed faithful to his mission to this very point. Even now, has she still faith in that mission? If so, what does she expect will happen? What do I?

The space between the thieves demands to be occupied. It urges the craftsman to continue his infuriatingly methodical work, finish the task, and go home. One of the thieves is shouting at Jesus: 'Aren't you the Christ? Get us down from here and save yourself!'

There are more from the temple now – chief priests and their cohorts, here to gloat at their success.

Psalm

From thee comes my praise in the great congregation; my vows I will pay before those who fear him.

Gospel

Luke 23:27–31

And there followed him a great multitude of the people, and of women who bewailed and lamented him. But Jesus turning to them said, 'Daughters of Jerusalem, do not weep for me, but weep for yourselves and for your children. For behold, the days are coming when they will say, "Blessed are the barren, and the wombs that never bore, and the breasts that never gave suck!" Then they will begin to say to the mountains, "Fall on us"; and to the hills, "Cover us." For if they do this when the wood is green, what will happen when it is dry?'

Comment

Luke brings into those who come to Calvary, not only the mockers, and the voyeurs, and the soldiers and those weeping women of Jerusalem, but the friends of Jesus and the women who had come with him from Galilee. They were to take their places at a distance from the cross. And if we are honest that is where we, each one of us, is likely to be found. Were the weeping women 'official' bewailers of the condemned man's sin? Were they loyal followers distraught at the fate of their Master? Were they guilty of collaborating with the baying and fickle crowds?

For further consideration . . .

'Weep for yourselves. Weep as the foolish virgins might weep when they are told: "You may not come in, I do not know you." Weep for yourselves: prepare for the things to come.'

Saturday 5

Looking at Jesus, the mocking, the stripping and the scourging done, I can see that he has collected and accepted and been crucified with all the vile venom and vehemence that can be mustered. The chief priests and elders are heaping this upon him on behalf of everyone else. A thief is swearing again and someone is silencing him. Soon he will be silent to this world.

The craftsman, apparently savouring his final act before the now larger crowd – for effect, I believe – is trying to decide between a long-shafted nail and two shorter ones. Which shall he choose? he wonders. I wonder. He is now studying the feet of the Master and kneels beside them, and is now positioning the right upon the left, causing the right leg to be fixed at an awkward and painful angle. He is placing the long nail on the right foot and raising his hammer.

Psalm

The afflicted shall eat and be satisfied; those who seek him shall praise the Lord! May your hearts live for ever!

Gospel

Luke 23:32
Mark 14:22–4

Two others also, who were criminals, were led away to be put to death with him. And they brought him to the place called Golgotha (which means the place of a skull). And they offered him wine mingled with myrrh; but he did not take it. And they crucified him, and divided his garments among them, casting lots for them, to decide what each should take.

Comment

God gives himself completely and goes to the uttermost, and empties himself in love and humility. The weakness and nakedness of the child of Bethlehem shows us the same love as the scourged and naked man to be nailed to the rough wood of the cross.

For further consideration . . .

It is appropriate now to consider the Incarnation paralleled by our Lord's real presence in the Blessed Sacrament.

Holy Week

FLESH
BONE
WOOD

Monday of Holy Week

The Centurion:

I have seen many an execution. This man in the middle is a rather different kettle of fish. He is not a run-of-the-mill criminal. Even the Jewish authorities have stirred up a fuss because the Governor insisted on wording the indictment personally. The Jews wanted this death. Why? It strikes me as odd. The fellow was a decent sort. Indeed, a colleague had some dealings with him: I believe this man cured his servant of some ailment or other. It strikes me as odd. He seems to have preached that the Jewish God was a paternal God who cared for all his creation. (Dare I think that the Roman Gods are make-believe and the art of the ingenious sculptor?) Why should their temple staff be so determined to rid themselves of him? They could have used him to good effect, I should have thought. Perhaps they recognized the truth of what he preached and what he was, and were frightened. I know what fear can do – fear of all types.

I see his mother there: she is comforting him by her presence. I shall have to stay to the end, there is something remarkable about it all and I've seen many a crucifixion.

Psalm

All the ends of the earth shall remember and turn
to the Lord; and all the families of the nations
shall worship before him.

Gospel

Mark 15:25
Luke 23:35–8

*And it was the third hour, when they crucified
him. And Jesus said, 'Father, forgive them; for
they know not what they do.' And they cast lots
to divide his garments. And the people stood by,
watching; but the rulers scoffed at him, saying,
'He saved others; let him save himself, if he is the
Christ of God, his Chosen One!' The soldiers also
mocked him, coming up and offering him vinegar,
and saying, 'If you are the King of the Jews, save
yourself!' There was also an inscription over him,
'This is the King of the Jews.'*

Comment

Jesus' kingship and authority is the kingship and authority of love. He redeems through suffering; he makes himself vulnerable, shares our weakness, that he might raise us up to share in his life, and live by his same love. The king enthroned on the cross comes into his kingdom of love, and we are those who are called to live by the laws of love in that kingdom.

For further consideration . . .

For the moment, the centurion stands aloof. Something will shortly nudge him.

Tuesday of Holy Week

The Beloved Disciple:

And so, three last hammer blows: 'Flesh! Bone! Wood!' No longer does my memory need to be prompted by the past. The hammer now tells us of the reality of the passage of the nail as it penetrates the flesh and pushes the bones aside and secures itself in the wood. The Master is there, pinned to a tree. Soon the craftsman will gather his tools into his hide bag and leave the scene, a job well done.

The centurion, almost in sorrow – but I daresay my eyes imagine it – is now directing his soldiers to rope the cross, guide the foot, and haul. The cross is rising slowly, for it carries a greater burden than the weight of the Master, and now drops into its shaft with a jolt. Jesus stretches his neck and closes his eyes for a moment. The three crosses are together.

I am moving forward with Mary to the foot of the cross: the other Marys and Salome are moving also.

Psalm

For dominion belongs to the Lord, and he rules over the nations.

Gospel

John 19:20-2

Many of the Jews read this title, for the place where Jesus was crucified was near the city; and it was written in Hebrew, in Latin, and in Greek. The chief priests of the Jews then said to Pilate, 'Do not write, "The King of the Jews", but, "This man said, I am King of the Jews."' Pilate answered, 'What I have written I have written.'

Comment

The label informs everyone: it is written in the language of the learned man of the temple; of the Roman; of the common man. Pilate, who has washed his hands of Jesus and of the truth, decrees that the label should be left as he has drafted it.

The cross of a criminal is the throne of Jesus' tortured body.

For further consideration . . .

Language is no barrier to the declaration of kingship: there is no barrier between the cross and humankind.

Wednesday of Holy Week

Does despair create fantasy? Is the Master not the epitome of a king, reigning over us from on high? Few would see it: his followers' tears do not support it. Having been lifted high on the cross on earth, shall he be lifted high in heaven? That is where he is going – to the Father, where we cannot yet follow.

The less aggressive thief has just admonished the other and has said to Jesus: 'Remember me when you come into your kingdom.' He is replying: 'Today, you shall be with me in Paradise.' Does that mean more than a relief from pain? Can a thief travel with him where a disciple cannot? Will there be work for us to do here without the Master?

Mary is looking up at her son and he returns the gaze and is addressing her with difficulty. 'Mother, look, your son,' he is saying, as he turns his head towards me adding: 'Look, your mother.'

Psalm

Yea to him shall all the proud of the earth bow down; before him shall bow all who go down to the dust, and he who cannot keep himself alive.

Gospel

Luke 23:39–43

One of the criminals who were hanged railed at him, saying, 'Are you not the Christ? Save yourself and us!' But the other rebuked him, saying, 'Do you not fear God, since you are under the same sentence of condemnation? And we indeed justly, for we are receiving the due reward of our deeds; but this man has done nothing wrong.' And he said, 'Jesus, remember me when you come in your kingly power.' And he said to him, 'Truly, I say to you, today you will be with me in Paradise.'

Comment

We are wounded disciples following a wounded Saviour, but we follow in the power of his Spirit who is the transfigurer of our wounds. 'There is no such thing as an unscarred saint,' wrote Father Andrew of the Society of the Divine Compassion. And wounds, which we all have, have only two things to be done to them – to be allowed to fester,

or to be offered to be cauterized and transfigured
in the healing love of Christ.

For further consideration . . .

Hanging next to God the Son, the thief asks to be
remembered. He asks only that. He does not
aspire any higher. He is rewarded with more.
How full of meaning is 'remember me'?

Maundy Thursday

I am to care for her as my own mother. I shall do so: how could I not? I place my arm around his mother to show him my response. He bleeds over the remnant of his followers and over his mother, now my mother.

Even at this late stage there are cries, cruel and mocking cries, from officialdom and the others who wish to enjoy the end. The Master is in prayer to the Father and I hear him recite a psalm that begins by recalling despair and ends in gladness. Each of his final moments seems to have a purpose in providing the finishing touches to his ministry. He now thirsts and is saying as much, and someone is offering him the traditional sponge of sour wine held to his lips on a stake. It is said to dull the pain. His devoted follower Mary of Magdala is crying copiously as she senses that the Master is making his final preparations.

Psalm

Posterity shall serve him; men shall tell of the Lord to the coming generation.

Gospel

John 19:26, 27

When Jesus saw his mother, and the disciple whom he loved standing near, he said to his mother, 'Woman, behold, your son!' Then he said to the disciple, 'Behold, your mother!' And from that hour the disciple took her to his own house.

Comment

Christian devotion through the ages has set the cross, in many different forms, on altar and on steeple. The cross is planted at the very heart of our faith. It is *the* Christian sign, and a Christianity without the cross is no Christianity at all. The early Christians looked around the world and, with the eye of faith, saw the cross imprinted on the very fabric of human lives, and on the world as God's creation. They looked at ships crossing the sea and saw the mast and yard-arm from which the sail hung, as the figure of the cross; they looked at their primitive ploughs and saw again the figure of the cross; they looked into the heavens and saw the planets and stars revolving against each other as forming the figure of a cross. They meditated on barriers between heaven and earth and Jew and Gentile as forming a cross, which Christ had transformed from a cross of separation into one that united.

For further consideration . . .

The complete and all-embracing love for human-kind is summed up in 'Behold, your Mother'.

Good Friday

Mary:

My son, my son, I am here. I am with you. But why this suffering; why such a death? I cannot bear it. Is this your Father's business which Joseph and I failed to understand when we lost you all those years ago in the temple?

I have prayed to the Father, but how can he be named as a loving Father and called 'Abba' when this is what happens, this torture, this bleeding, this racking of pain? And yet, and yet, I still hold on to that promise at your coming and still I whisper the response of faith: Be it unto me according to your word. And still I ask: Lord, I believe, help my unbelief.

First Thief:

O the pain, the agony. Let's get it over with quickly. Hardly worth it, that stuff we pinched. It wasn't so very much we'd taken, and they get rid of us like this, lumped together with this crazy kid who thinks he's some kind of a prophet. How's it feel now? Stupid fool!

Second Thief:

For heaven's sake don't make it worse. You never know with these blokes . . . might have something . . . Lord, remember me when you come into your kingdom.

Our Lord:

Father, forgive them, they do not know what they are doing. Father, if it be your will, let this cup pass from me, nevertheless not my will but yours be done. Father, the darkness presses upon me: the darkness of the sky, the darkness of this pain, the darkness of betrayal, loneliness, abandonment. Father, how dark, how heavy is this weight of evil. Father, your love is the light of life, but where are you? Where is that love, that knowledge of your presence, that delight in your care? My God, my God, I cry to you in agony and pain, out of the depths of hell, from the darkness of death. My God, my God, why have you forsaken me? With pierced hands and feet, with wounded heart, out of the deep I call to you O Lord, Lord, hear my voice. Lord, I thirst, thirst for your presence, my Father, for all you have given me, for the life of the world. Into your hands I commend my spirit, for it is finished, perfected, completed.

The Beloved Disciple:

Mary is resolute. She will remain until he breathes his last and is taken down for burial. I shall remain with her. A few moments ago he cried out and said that his mission was complete. It becomes clearer to me as time passes that this really must be part of it, though there is no feeling of triumph and success in my soul. We had no wish to contemplate the uncomfortable and the unpleasant when he gave those warnings and accurate predictions.

The craftsman is on his way homeward. The thieves are quiet but still a long way from death; the Master is close to it. He is opening his mouth to speak and is summoning up strength. He is commending himself to God. His head now droops and I think he is dead. Mary's head droops also. There is a numbness, a blankness, though everything around me is the same. The bodies will be removed quickly after the soldiers have made sure that all are dead.

The centurion has made an unexpected remark, which reminds me that, at the Master's baptism in the Jordan, a voice from heaven said roughly the same thing.

Psalm

And proclaim his deliverance to a people yet unborn, that he has wrought it.

Gospel

Mark 15:33, 34
John 19:28, 29
Luke 23:46

And when the sixth hour had come, there was darkness over the whole land until the ninth hour. And at the ninth hour Jesus cried with a loud voice, 'Eloi, Eloi, lama sabachthani?' which means, 'My God, my God, why hast thou forsaken me?'

After this Jesus, knowing that all was now finished, said (to fulfil the scripture), 'I thirst.' A bowl full of vinegar stood there, so they put a sponge full of the vinegar on hyssop and held it to his mouth. Then Jesus, crying with a loud voice, said, 'Father, into thy hands I commit my spirit!' And having said this he breathed his last.

Comment

As we stand on the hill of Calvary and edge towards the foot of the cross, we look at our Lord hanging there in agony and pain. That is the mirror for us of the love of God. God loves and cares for us, so individually, in all our needs, in our weakness and in our strength, that he enters into our condition and knows it from the inside. He redeems through suffering; he makes himself vulnerable, shares our weakness, that he might raise us up to share in his life, and live by his same love. The Christ who died is the Christ who was raised to life for us, and is raised to life in us: Good Friday and Easter belong together.

For further consideration . . .

We can consider matters only in the knowledge of the Resurrection and our redemption because we are Easter people.

Prayer

Lord, you were nailed to the cross for love of me. You knew from the inside our human pain, our burden of sin, the world's evil. You knew injustice, betrayal and abandonment. You knew, like us, the absence of your Father in the darkness, and yet in that darkness he was with you, so that out of every hell you have redeemed mankind. We adore you, O Christ, and we bless you because by your Holy Cross you have redeemed the world. You Christ are the King of Glory, crowned with thorns you reign in triumph, lifted high on the cross. We worship your great love and praise you for your glory. Amen.

Holy Saturday

Jesus is dead. A soldier has just made sure of it with the thrust of his spear, the spear whose shaft restrained Mary and restrained me earlier in the day. With sickening barbarity, the others are being finished off.

The miracle in Cana again comes to mind. That was his beginning and this his end. The outpouring of water into wine warned of the outpouring of the cup of wine not so many hours ago and of his blood today. Is there comfort in that? Not yet. We are bereft and there is now a hollowness and emptiness. When will the owner of the vineyard come to exact revenge?

We shall bury the Master and lay the temple that is his body in a tomb, there to remain . . .

Psalm 93

The floods have lifted up, O Lord, the floods have lifted up their voice, the floods lift up their roaring. Mightier than the thunders of many waters, mightier than the waves of the sea, the Lord on high is mighty!

Gospel

John 19:33–7, 40–2

But when they came to Jesus and saw that he was already dead, they did not break his legs. But one of the soldiers pierced his side with a spear, and at once there came out blood and water. He who saw it has borne witness – his testimony is true, and he knows that he tells the truth – that you also may believe. For these things took place that the scripture might be fulfilled. 'Not a bone of him shall be broken.' And again another scripture says, 'They shall look on him whom they have pierced.' They took the body of Jesus, and bound it in linen cloths with the spices, as is the burial custom of the Jews. Now in the place where he was crucified there was a garden, and in the garden a new tomb where no one had ever been laid. So because of the Jewish day of Preparation, as the tomb was close at hand, they laid Jesus there.

Comment

Today, Holy Saturday, or Easter Eve, is surely the most mysterious day of the Christian calendar, and yet all too rarely do Christians pause to consider its significance. Time, thought and energy are taken up with the decoration of churches for Easter. Poised between the darkness of Good Friday and the light of Easter, it is a day of profound silence. 'Christ suffered, died and was buried.' Today the Christ of God is with the dead, eliminated from the world, knowing death as completely and absolutely as each one of us will eventually know death.

The Gospel records of the Passion tell of the agony of Gethsemane – a shrinking from the costly demand of redemptive love. They speak of a darkness over the land on Good Friday that is more than physical, a dark inner engulfing of meaning and purpose. They place on the lips of Jesus the powerful opening of Psalm 22; a psalm that goes on to speak of the desiccating torture as life ebbs away.

He not only died, the creed affirms that 'he descended into hell'. Strictly, this is Hades (or the Hebrew *She'ol*) the place of wraith-like existence of the departed. Part of the stumbling-block of Christianity is that the God who was revealed in the particularity of the life of Jesus is a God who goes to the uttermost into the very nothingness of death. And God goes into that nothingness through a descent into the hell of unmeaning. The cry of dereliction on the lips of the crucified is terrifying. If incarnation is real, if God engages so radically with the world as to know the world's evil and our human mortality from the inside,

God chooses to experience and encompass a world without God and so without ultimate meaning. He descended into the hell that is apartness from God; into the hell of the absence of God; into the hell of impotent rage against God; into the silence of the grave. The twisted, tortured figure clamped by crude nails to the wood of the cross is where the God who is love goes to the uttermost. There the evil and suffering of the world which was created with the terrible freedom to love and to deny love is known from the inside. Here, says Lancelot Andrewes, 'the very book of charity is laid open before us'.

In the nineteenth century G. W. F. Hegel wrote that 'the human, the finite, the fragile, the weak, the negative are themselves a moment of the divine; they are within God himself'. The psalmist, centuries earlier, had reached out in faith to affirm, 'If I go down to hell, thou art there also.' In the early centuries of the Church, the Christian imagination sought to express in vivid pictures this free choosing of God to know and be found in the darkness. The apocryphal Gospel of Nicodemus dramatically describes the encounter in the realm of the dead between Christ and the powers of darkness who held the departed captive. The walls of hell fall like the walls of Jericho and the prisoners are set free. Here is the basis for the harrowing-of-hell scenes in countless mediaeval passion plays in which the archetypal conflict of good and evil, of life and death, is as popular as it is in the cinema of the twentieth century.

'He descended into hell' – the silence of Holy Saturday takes Good Friday to the uttermost, and it is from that silence of the grave, and the darkness of evil triumphant, that Christ is raised to the life of God's new creation. History is broken open to the life of the world to come, and the reign of the love that death could not hold is the kingdom of God that the Easter Gospel proclaims. The ikons of Eastern Christendom portray the Resurrection not, as in mediaeval Western painting, showing Christ stepping out of a tomb, but as Christ's triumph over the imprisoning powers of darkness. One of the most powerful of these images, in the church of St Saviour in Chora in Istanbul, shows Christ in a shimmering mandala of glory with hands outstretched drawing Adam and Eve, representing all humanity, from death to life, from the old order to the new. Beneath his feet the bolts and bars of hell lie shattered. The prisoners are set free, the demons are fallen, and life reigns. It is no wonder that in St Mark's Gospel the women run from the empty tomb in terror.

For further consideration . . .

To what extent do our words and deeds equate with the thrust of the spear?

The Day of Resurrection

CHRIST
IS
RISEN

O the fair beauty of earth, from the
death of the winter arising
Every good gift of the year now
with its Master returns.

Easter Morning

It is likely that most of Jesus' disciples would have dispersed into hiding after the crucifixion, but by Sunday morning, we know that at least some were together. Had they been rallied by the Beloved Disciple and had he given them accounts of his experiences beside the cross? After all, we know from Luke that Jesus' followers were standing at some distance from the cross. It is not difficult to believe, however, that a few had perhaps briefly moved forward, nervously, reluctantly and even sheepishly, to witness the removal of Jesus' body from the cross.

Immediately after the rather hurried burial, the women must have made plans to return to the tomb after the Sabbath in order to conclude the rite of anointing and cleansing the body. In what spirit was that Sabbath celebrated?

On the Sunday morning the disciples were undoubtedly still confused and despondent and unlikely to have been harbouring expectations of Jesus' resurrection. They had heard our Lord's words often enough, but there was as yet no comprehension. Following the visits to the tomb, word spread among the disciples and we know from St John's Gospel that only Thomas was absent from their number on Sunday evening.

Gospel

Mark 8:31, 32a; 9:31b–32; 10:33b, 34; 16:1–8

And he began to teach them that the Son of man must suffer many things, and be rejected by the elders and the chief priests and the scribes, and be killed, and after three days rise again. And he said this plainly.

'The Son of man will be delivered into the hands of men, and they will kill him; and when he is killed, after three days, he will rise.' But they did not understand the saying, and they were afraid to ask him.

'The Son of man will be delivered to the chief priests and the scribes, and they will condemn him to death, and deliver him to the Gentiles, and they will mock him, and spit upon him, and scourge him, and kill him; and after three days he will rise.'

And when the Sabbath was past, Mary Magdalene, and Mary, the mother of James, and Salome, bought spices, so that they might go and anoint him. And very early on the first day of the week they went to the tomb when the sun had risen. And they were saying to one another, 'Who will roll away the stone for us from the door of the tomb?' And looking up, they saw that the stone was rolled back; for it was very large. And entering the tomb, they saw a young man sitting on the right side, dressed in a white robe; and they were amazed. And he said to them, 'Do not be amazed; you seek Jesus of Nazareth, who was crucified. He has risen, he is not here; see the place where they laid him. But go, tell his disciples and Peter that he is going before you to Galilee; there you will see him, as he told you.' And they went out and fled from the tomb; for trembling and astonishment had come upon them; and they said nothing to any one, for they were afraid.

Comment

St Mark's Gospel may well have ended in this way with the women running away from the tomb. They were afraid; they were frightened out of their wits; they were overcome with awe. In the original Greek, the abruptness of the seemingly unfinished ending is even more striking as it actually concludes with the word 'for'. Is Mark saying: 'Well, you know the rest'? After all, he was writing in full knowledge of and belief in the Resurrection, and probably to those who themselves believed firmly. However, some scholars think that perhaps Mark's original ending found its way into St John's Gospel. In that Gospel, Mary Magdalene runs to bring news of the Resurrection to the others. And on Easter evening, the Risen Lord appears to the frightened disciples, greets them and breathes on them the gift of nothing less than his own life.

Easter is an explosion – a stunning, overwhelming, surprising event which blows our human history wide open, and transforms our expectations. *Dead men are dead. Bodies rot in the ground. When a life is over, the person may live in our memory but that is all.* But Easter is not like that; it turns the world upside-down, for God has done a new thing, a surpassing, wonderful, new thing. It is not surprising that Gospel accounts of the Resurrection of Jesus are all clear that something new and surprising has happened, but that the accounts stumble and vary over the details. Who goes to the tomb first? Who first encounters the Risen Jesus? There are appearances in Jerusalem and appearances in Galilee. And yet, all the Easter stories in the Gospels (and St Paul's witness in his letters) home in on one single, rich, and amazing truth – Christ is risen and Jesus is alive. The cross is not, therefore, the end, because death is conquered. This Resurrection, this new life, this new creation, is a life to be shared.

The poet Gerard Manley Hopkins talks about Christ 'Eastering' in us. That reminds us powerfully that Easter – the Resurrection – is for Christians something active, alive and transforming and not something rather odd and strange that happened in the past. Easter life is something we share here and now, but something we share in that its completeness only at the final fulfilment of God's purposes. St Paul puts it thus: 'As in Adam all die, so in Christ shall all be made alive.' Easter, for all the Gospels, is not just about Jesus but about the disciples; not just about all the disciples but about all Christians; not just about all Christians but about us. From now on we are Easter people and Alleluia (Praise be to God) is our song.

> *Alleluia, Christ is Risen!*
> *He is risen indeed, Alleluia!*

Prayer

Christ, who is sinless, reconciles sinners to the Father. Death and life have contended in that combat stupendous: the Prince of Life, who died, reigns immortal. Christ indeed from death is risen, our new life securing: have mercy, victor King, ever reigning. Amen. Alleluia.

(*from the Easter Sequence*)

O Risen Lord, secure in me the knowledge of your forgiving mercy, the comfort of your redeeming love and the joy of your all-powerful Resurrection from the dead. And give me the strength to take up my cross and follow you to the heavenly realms where you reign in glory with the Father and the Holy Spirit throughout all ages. Amen.

Psalm

The Lord reigns; he is robed in majesty; the Lord is robed, he is girded with strength. Yea, the world is established; it shall never be moved, thy throne is established from of old; thou art from everlasting. Thy decrees are very sure; holiness befits thy house, O Lord, for evermore.